1,000 AMAZING WORLD FACTS

SECOND EDITION
DK Delhi
Assistant art editor Diya Varma
Senior picture researcher Sumedha Chopra
Deputy managing art editor Shreya Anand
Managing art editor Govind Mittal
Production editor Jaypal Singh Chauhan
Jacket designer Juhi Sheth
DTP designers Mrinmoy Mazumdar, Anita Yadav
DTP coordinator Vishal Bhatia
Senior jackets Coordinator Priyanka Sharma Saddic

DK London
Senior editor Shaila Brown
Senior US editor Kayla Dugger
Executive US editor Lori Cates Hand
Senior art editor Jacqui Swan
Managing editor Rachel Fox
Managing art editor Owen Peyton Jones
Production controller Laura Andrews
Jacket designer Akiko Kato
Jacket design development manager Sophia MTT
Publisher Andrew Macintyre
Associate publishing director Liz Wheeler
Art director Karen Self
Publishing director Jonathan Metcalf

Contributor Andrea Mills

Content previously published in *It Can't Be True!*

FIRST EDITION
Senior editor Rob Houston
Editors Helen Abramson, Wendy Horobin,
Steve Setford, Rona Skene
Designers David Ball, Peter Laws,
Clare Marshall, Anis Sayyed, Jemma Westing
Illustrators Adam Benton, Stuart Jackson-Carter,
Anders Kjellberg, Simon Mumford
Creative retouching Steve Willis
Picture research Aditya Katyal, Martin Copeland
Jacket design Jessica Bentall,
Laura Brim, Jemma Westing
Jacket editor Manisha Majithia
Jacket design development manager
Sophia M. Tampakopoulos Turner
Producer (pre-production) Rebekah Parsons-King
Production controller Mandy Inness
Managing art editor Philip Letsu
Managing editor Gareth Jones
Publisher Andrew Macintyre
Art director Phil Ormerod
Associate publishing director Liz Wheeler
Publishing director Jonathan Metcalf

Author Andrea Mills

This American Edition, 2024
First American Edition, 2013
Published in the United States by DK Publishing
1745 Broadway, 20th Floor, New York, NY 10019

Copyright © 2013, 2024 Dorling Kindersley Limited
DK, a Division of Penguin Random House LLC
24 25 26 27 28 10 9 8 7 6 5 4 3 2 1
001–339258–March/2024

A catalog record for this book is available
from the Library of Congress.
ISBN 978-0-7440-9286-8

Printed and bound in China

www.dk.com

CONTENTS

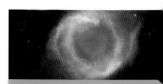

1 Out of this world

2 Astounding Earth

3 Humans and other life forms

4 Feats of engineering

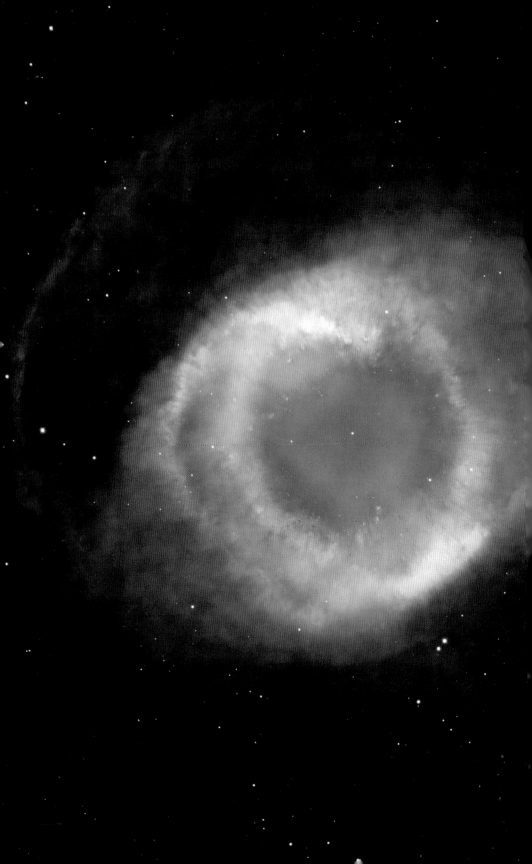

Out of this world

Beyond the safety of planet Earth, space is an incredibly hostile place—vast, airless, and unimaginably cold. But space is also full of amazing things, from fiery stars and weird worlds to mysterious moons, blazing comets, and hurtling asteroids.

The Helix Nebula is made up of huge shells of gas and dust thrown off by a dying star. It is expanding at a rate of nearly 72,000 mph (115,000 kph), which is around 15 times the speed of the fastest-ever aircraft, the rocket-powered North American X-15.

HOW BIG IS
THE SUN?

The average **diameter** of the **Sun** is **864,337 miles** (1,391,016 km). It is **333,000 times** the mass of **Earth.**

You could fit 109 Earths across the diameter of the Sun.

SUNSPOTS

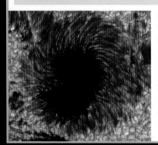

Sunspots are areas where a strong magnetic field stops hot gas from reaching the surface. When sunspot numbers increase every 11 years, the Sun's intense magnetic activity can affect radio signals on Earth.

THE SUN IS ABOUT 4.6 BILLION YEARS OLD. IT WILL SHINE FOR ANOTHER 5 BILLION YEARS.

ENERGY FROM THE SUN'S CORE CAN TAKE AT LEAST 100,000 YEARS TO REACH THE SURFACE.

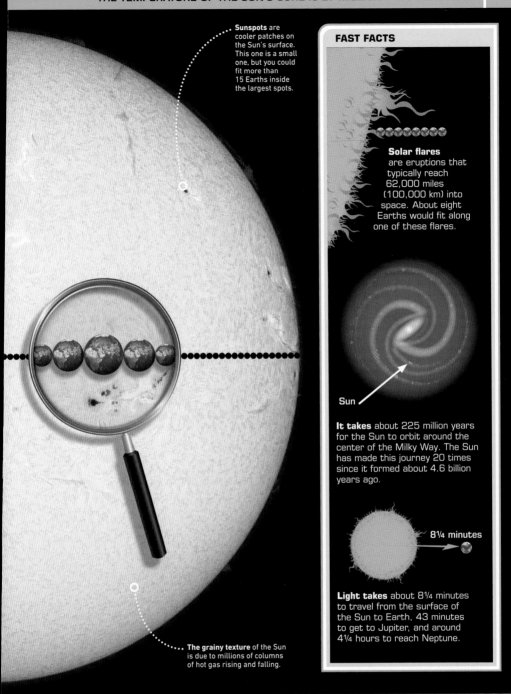

Sunspots are cooler patches on the Sun's surface. This one is a small one, but you could fit more than 15 Earths inside the largest spots.

FAST FACTS

Solar flares are eruptions that typically reach 62,000 miles (100,000 km) into space. About eight Earths would fit along one of these flares.

Sun

It takes about 225 million years for the Sun to orbit around the center of the Milky Way. The Sun has made this journey 20 times since it formed about 4.6 billion years ago.

8¼ minutes

Light takes about 8¼ minutes to travel from the surface of the Sun to Earth, 43 minutes to get to Jupiter, and around 4¼ hours to reach Neptune.

The grainy texture of the Sun is due to millions of columns of hot gas rising and falling.

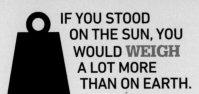

IF YOU STOOD ON THE SUN, YOU WOULD WEIGH A LOT MORE THAN ON EARTH.

THE STAR VY CANIS MAJORIS IS EVEN BIGGER THAN THE SUN—3 BILLION SUNS COULD FIT INSIDE IT.

HOW BIG IS
THE MOON?

The **Moon's diameter** is **2,159 miles** (3,475 km), **one-quarter** the size of **Earth's.** Its surface area is **13 times smaller**.

The **Copernicus Crater**, one of the Moon's largest, measures 58 miles (93 km) across.

A PERFECT FIT

The Sun is 400 times the diameter of the Moon, but by an amazing coincidence, it is also 400 times farther from Earth. This means that, seen from Earth during an eclipse, the Sun and the Moon appear exactly the same size.

Australia

THE MOON APPEARS TO SHINE AT NIGHT, BUT IT DOES NOT PRODUCE ANY LIGHT— IT REFLECTS THE LIGHT OF THE SUN.

EARTHQUAKES ON THE MOON, KNOWN AS MOONQUAKES, CAN LAST FOR MORE THAN 10 MINUTES.

The Moon is the fifth-largest satellite in the Solar System, after three of Jupiter's moons and one of Saturn's. It is the Solar System's largest satellite relative to its planet. It doesn't usually hover above Australia, but orbits at a much more distant 238,854 miles (384,399 km) from Earth.

The Sea of Tranquility is a flat plain of lava that solidified around 4 billion years ago. It is a little larger than the British Isles.

The Moon is almost as wide as Australia, which is 2,475 miles (3,983 km) across at its widest point.

FAST FACTS

Earth measures 7,926 miles (12,756 km) across at the equator. Four Moons could line up across it.

If there were no gaps, 50 Moons could fit inside the globe.

It would take 80 Moons to balance the scales against one Earth. Earth is so much heavier because its core is made of iron and nickel and is as wide as two Moons.

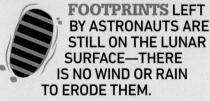

FOOTPRINTS LEFT BY ASTRONAUTS ARE STILL ON THE LUNAR SURFACE—THERE IS NO WIND OR RAIN TO ERODE THEM.

SCIENTISTS THINK THAT THE MOON HAS BEEN SHRINKING, FORMING WRINKLELIKE FEATURES CALLED THRUST FAULTS.

HOW BIG ARE THE
PLANETS?

The **planets** in our Solar System **vary in size**. Some are **small and rocky**, while others are **enormous balls of gas**.

POISONOUS VENUS

Venus is almost the same size and mass as Earth but is very different. Venus has a thick, poisonous atmosphere and a surface temperature of 867°F (464°C), which is hot enough to melt lead.

Jupiter, the biggest planet, measures 86,888 miles (139,833 km) across. It is made mainly of clouds of swirling gas.

Earth is 7,918 miles (12,742 km) in diameter on average, although like most planets, it is slightly fatter around the equator. It is the largest of the rocky planets.

URANUS IS THE COLDEST PLANET IN THE SOLAR SYSTEM—TEMPERATURES ARE AS LOW AS -371°F (-224°C).

SATURN'S RINGS WERE FIRST OBSERVED IN 1610 BY ITALIAN ASTRONOMER GALILEO GALILEI.

FAST FACTS

Venus and Uranus spin in the opposite direction to the other planets. Uranus also rotates on its side, so it appears to spin clockwise or counterclockwise depending on the pole you're looking at.

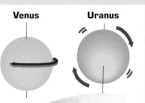

Venus   Uranus

Saturn is the second biggest planet at 72,367 miles (116,464 km) in diameter. It is made mainly of the gases hydrogen and helium.

Saturn's rings are made up of dust, rock, and ice. They extend 298,258 miles (480,000 km) but are only about 0.6 mile (1 km) thick.

Uranus is 31,518 miles (50,724 km) in diameter and is the farthest planet you can see with the naked eye. It is mostly made of gas, which surrounds a small, rocky core.

Neptune is made of very cold gas. The farthest planet from the Sun, it has a diameter of 30,599 miles (49,244 km).

Venus is a rocky planet and, at 7,521 miles (12,104 km) across, is nearly as big as Earth.

Mercury's diameter is 29 times smaller than Jupiter's.

Mars measures 4,212 miles (6,799 km) across. It is known as the "red planet" due to the color of its rusty, iron-rich rocks.

Mercury is the smallest planet, just 3,032 miles (4,879 km) across. It lies the closest to the Sun and is made of rock.

WITH WIND SPEEDS EXCEEDING 1,200 MPH (2,000 KPH), NEPTUNE IS THE WINDIEST PLANET IN THE SOLAR SYSTEM.

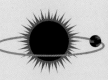

MERCURY ORBITS THE SUN FASTER THAN ANY PLANET IN THE SOLAR SYSTEM.

FAST FACTS

Although Saturn is the second biggest planet, it is not very dense. If you could fill a bathtub big enough with water, Saturn would float. All the other planets, including Jupiter, would sink to the bottom.

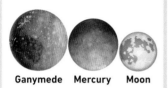

Ganymede Mercury Moon

Jupiter has at least 92 moons. The biggest, Ganymede, is also the largest moon in the Solar System. It is bigger than the planet Mercury and our own Moon.

Around 11 Earths would fit across Jupiter's diameter.

Jupiter is made largely of gas, with a small, rocky core. It is around two and a half times the combined mass of all the other planets put together.

Bands of clouds are created as Jupiter spins. It rotates once every 10 hours, faster than all the other planets.

TURBULENT **CLOUDS** OF AMMONIA AND WATER SWIRL AROUND JUPITER AT SPEEDS OF UP TO 325 MPH (523 KPH).

JUPITER HAS THE SHORTEST DAY IN THE SOLAR SYSTEM— ONE DAY TAKES **10 HOURS**.

HOW BIG IS
JUPITER?

More than
1,320 Earths
would fit
inside Jupiter.

The **biggest planet** in the Solar System is **Jupiter.** It has a **diameter** of **86,888 miles** (139, 833 km); a **circumference** of **272,967 miles** (439,298 km); and a total **volume** of **343 trillion cu miles** (1,431 trillion cu km).

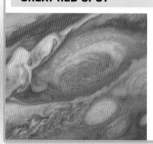

GREAT RED SPOT

The Great Red Spot is an enormous storm raging in the atmosphere of Jupiter. It is more than 12,427 miles (20,000 km) wide. You could fit two or three Earths inside it.

JUPITER'S **GRAVITY** IS 2.5 TIMES STRONGER THAN EARTH, SO YOU WOULD WEIGH 2.5 TIMES MORE ON JUPITER!

PRESSURE AT THE CENTER OF JUPITER IS EQUIVALENT TO ABOUT 160,000 CARS STACKED ON TOP YOU!

HOW BIG IS
AN ASTEROID?

This mountain is one of the tallest peaks in the Solar System.

Asteroids range from rocks **a few feet** (meters) across to the giants **Vesta (356 miles**/573 km across) and **Ceres (590 miles**/950 km across). **Ceres** is now also classed as a **dwarf planet.**

United States

CHELYABINSK METEOR

If an asteroid enters Earth's atmosphere, it is called a meteor. In 2013, a meteor about 56 ft (17 m) wide exploded over Russia, shattering windows and damaging buildings with its shockwave.

The chances of something the size of Vesta being on a collision course with Earth are very slim. If it did hit our planet, the impact would be so catastrophic that no life would survive. The asteroid that killed the dinosaurs 66 million years ago was no more than 9 miles (15 km) across.

CERES HAS A SURFACE AREA THAT IS ABOUT THE SAME AS THE SURFACE AREA OF INDIA.

CERES MAY HAVE WATER ICE BENEATH ITS SURFACE, WHICH MAY PROVIDE CLUES AS TO HOW EARTH GOT ITS OCEANS.

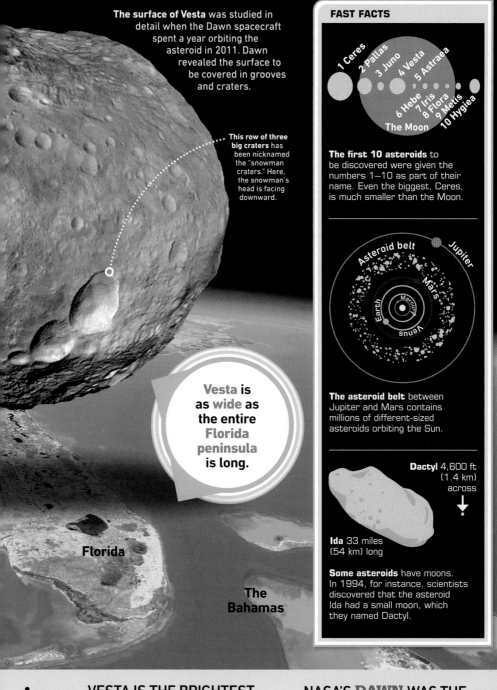

The surface of Vesta was studied in detail when the Dawn spacecraft spent a year orbiting the asteroid in 2011. Dawn revealed the surface to be covered in grooves and craters.

This row of three big craters has been nicknamed the "snowman craters." Here, the snowman's head is facing downward.

Vesta is as wide as the entire Florida peninsula is long.

Florida

The Bahamas

FAST FACTS

1 Ceres 2 Pallas 3 Juno 4 Vesta 5 Astraea 6 Hebe 7 Iris 8 Flora 9 Metis 10 Hygiea
The Moon

The first 10 asteroids to be discovered were given the numbers 1–10 as part of their name. Even the biggest, Ceres, is much smaller than the Moon.

Asteroid belt Jupiter Mars Earth Mercury Venus

The asteroid belt between Jupiter and Mars contains millions of different-sized asteroids orbiting the Sun.

Dactyl 4,600 ft (1.4 km) across

Ida 33 miles (54 km) long

Some asteroids have moons. In 1994, for instance, scientists discovered that the asteroid Ida had a small moon, which they named Dactyl.

VESTA IS THE BRIGHTEST **ASTEROID** IN THE NIGHT SKY—IT CAN SOMETIMES BE SEEN FROM EARTH WITH THE NAKED EYE.

NASA'S **DAWN** WAS THE FIRST SPACECRAFT TO ORBIT TWO WORLDS: VESTA AND CERES.

HOW BIG IS
A COMET?

A comet's **nucleus** is **small**, but the **dust** and **gases** that surround it (the **coma**) can measure **62,000 miles** (100,000 km) across.

Jupiter
86,888 miles
(139,833 km) across

CRASH LANDING

Most comets go around the Sun, but some are captured by Jupiter's massive gravitational pull. In July 1994, the fragments of comet Shoemaker-Levy 9 slammed into Jupiter, leaving a line of dark spots where they hit its atmosphere.

A **COMET'S TAIL** CAN BE MANY MILLIONS OF MILES (KM) LONG.

WITH A DIAMETER OF 80 MILES (129 KM), COMET **BERNARDINELLI-BERNSTEIN** HAS THE LARGEST KNOWN NUCLEUS.

FAST FACTS

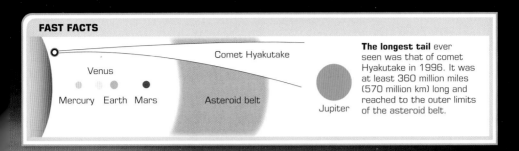

Comet Hyakutake

Venus

Mercury   Earth   Mars

Asteroid belt

Jupiter

The longest tail ever seen was that of comet Hyakutake in 1996. It was at least 360 million miles (570 million km) long and reached to the outer limits of the asteroid belt.

The nucleus of a comet usually measures less than 6 miles (10 km) in diameter. However, it is surrounded by an enormous coma of dust and gases.

A comet's coma can spread nearly as wide as Jupiter, the Solar System's largest planet.

Comets spend most of their lives as small, icy bodies orbiting in the outer regions of the Solar System. The orbits of some comets, however, send them hurtling inward. As a comet gets close to the Sun, its ice turns into gas and is blown away from the nucleus by the solar wind, forming a tail. Dust released from the comet creates a second tail, which stretches directly behind the comet.

ONE OF THE SMALLEST KNOWN COMETS, HARTLEY 2, HAS A DIAMETER OF ABOUT 1 MILE (1.6 KM).

IN 2014, ROSETTA-PHILAE BECAME THE FIRST CRAFT TO ORBIT A COMET WHEN IT REACHED 67P/C-G.

WHERE IS THE BIGGEST
CANYON?

The **Valles Marineris** on **Mars** is up to **4 miles** (7 km) **deep** and more than **2,500 miles** (4,000 km) **long**. America's **Grand Canyon** would fit along its length **nine times**.

If the **Valles Marineris** was in North America, it would stretch from the **Atlantic** to the **Pacific**.

Noctis Labyrinthus

Melas Chasma

2,500 miles

GRAND CANYON SKYWALK

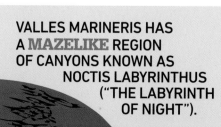

The Grand Canyon Skywalk is a transparent viewing platform. Visitors can see through the walkway to the bottom of the canyon 4,000 ft (1,200 m) below.

VALLES MARINERIS HAS A MAZELIKE REGION OF CANYONS KNOWN AS NOCTIS LABYRINTHUS ("THE LABYRINTH OF NIGHT").

MORE WATER-RELATED MINERALS HAVE BEEN DISCOVERED IN NOCTIS LABYRINTHUS THAN ANYWHERE ELSE ON MARS.

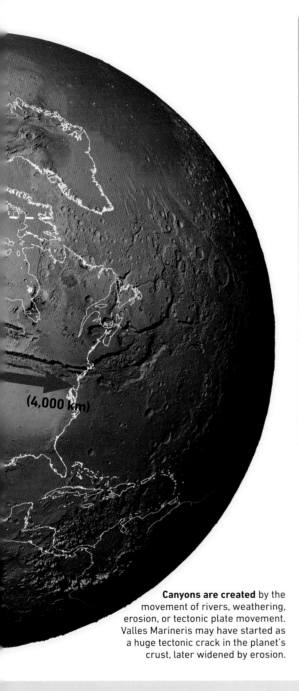

(4,000 km)

Canyons are created by the movement of rivers, weathering, erosion, or tectonic plate movement. Valles Marineris may have started as a huge tectonic crack in the planet's crust, later widened by erosion.

FAST FACTS

0 ft

3,280 ft (1,000 m)

6,560 ft (2,000 m)

9,840 ft (3,000 m)

13,120 ft (4,000 m)

16,400 ft (5,000 m)

19,680 ft (6,000 m)

22,970 ft (7,000 m)

26,247 ft (8,000 m)

Valles Marineris (Mars)
22,965 ft (7,000 m)

Yarlung Tsangpo (Tibet, China)
19,715 ft (6,009 m)

Colca Canyon (Peru)
13,650 ft (4,160 m)

Grand Canyon (US)
6,093 ft (1,857 m)

The deepest known canyons on Earth are the Yarlung Tsangpo and the Kali Gandaki (in Nepal).

Yarlung Tsangpo (Tibet, China)
308 miles (496 km)

Grand Canyon (US)
277 miles (445 km)

Hells Canyon (US)
125 miles (201 km)

Fish River Canyon (Namibia)
100 miles (160 km)

The longest canyon on Earth, the Yarlung Tsangpo, is also the world's biggest. It was carved by the Yarlung Tsangpo river, which becomes the Brahmaputra river when it later flows through India.

THE **DEEPEST** SECTION OF THE CANYON IS THE MELAS CHASMA. IT IS ALSO THE WIDEST AREA.

DUST STORMS THAT SHAPE VALLES MARINERIS ARE SO HUGE, THEY CAN BE SEEN BY TELESCOPE FROM EARTH.

Solar System data

How long would it take a plane traveling at 560 mph (900 kph) to **reach each planet from the Sun?**

THE SIZE
OF THE SOLAR SYSTEM
is equal to
100,000
times the distance from the Sun to Earth.

Traveling at 186,282 miles per second (299,792 km per second), sunlight takes **8 minutes and 20 seconds** to reach Earth from the Sun and **555.5 days** to reach the edge of the Solar System.

A **LONG** DAY
Because Mercury spins very slowly and orbits so close to the Sun, its day (measuring 176 Earth days) is actually **longer** than its year, which lasts for 87.97 Earth days.

COMETS
The nucleus of a comet can range in size from **80 to 25 miles** (129 to 40 km)

Comets formed at the same time as the rest of the Solar System, around
4.6
billion years ago. Like the planets, comets orbit the Sun.

When a comet gets near the Sun, its nucleus begins to melt, forming a **tail** of gas and dust that can **stretch** for **millions of miles** (km).

MERCURY 7.4 years

VENUS 13.7 years

EARTH 18.9 years

MARS 28.9 years

JUPITER 98.7 years

SATURN 180.9 years

URANUS 364.1 years

NEPTUNE 570.5 years

DAY LENGTH
A **day** is measured as the **time** it takes for a planet to **spin once on its axis** so that the Sun returns to the same spot in the sky.

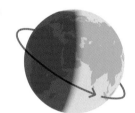

Mercury: 176 Earth days
Venus: 117 Earth days
Mars: 24 hr 40 min
Jupiter: 9 hr 56 min
Saturn: 10 hr 33 min
Uranus: 17 hr 14 min
Neptune: 16 hr 6 min

This list measures day length in Earth days, hours, and minutes.

THE FIRST WOMAN IN SPACE WAS RUSSIAN VALENTINA TERESHKOVA. IN 1963, SHE SPENT **3 DAYS** ORBITING EARTH.

ROSETTA-PHILAE WAS THE FIRST CRAFT TO ORBIT A COMET. ITS MISSION LASTED OVER **12 YEARS**.

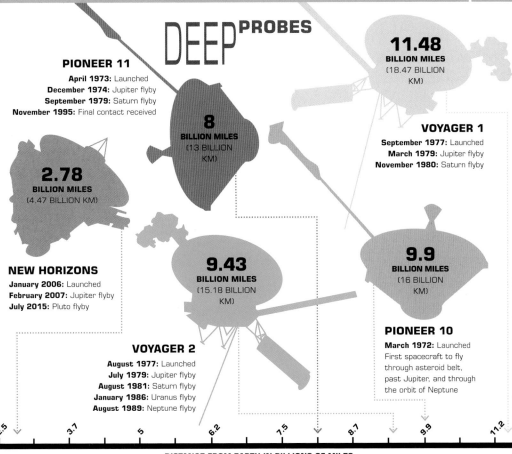

DEEP PROBES

PIONEER 11

April 1973: Launched
December 1974: Jupiter flyby
September 1979: Saturn flyby
November 1995: Final contact received

8
BILLION MILES
(13 BILLION KM)

11.48
BILLION MILES
(18.47 BILLION KM)

VOYAGER 1

September 1977: Launched
March 1979: Jupiter flyby
November 1980: Saturn flyby

2.78
BILLION MILES
(4.47 BILLION KM)

NEW HORIZONS

January 2006: Launched
February 2007: Jupiter flyby
July 2015: Pluto flyby

9.43
BILLION MILES
(15.18 BILLION KM)

9.9
BILLION MILES
(16 BILLION KM)

PIONEER 10

March 1972: Launched
First spacecraft to fly
through asteroid belt,
past Jupiter, and through
the orbit of Neptune

VOYAGER 2

August 1977: Launched
July 1979: Jupiter flyby
August 1981: Saturn flyby
January 1986: Uranus flyby
August 1989: Neptune flyby

2.5　3.7　5　6.2　7.5　8.7　9.9　11.2

DISTANCE FROM EARTH IN BILLIONS OF MILES

DWARF PLANETS

As well as the eight large planets, the Solar System is also home to a number of smaller objects known as **dwarf planets**. The biggest discovered so far are:

Eris: radius
723 miles (1,163 km)

Pluto: radius
715 miles (1,151 km)

Makemake: radius
441 miles (710 km)

EXO PLANETS

Ours is not the only solar system. Other stars are also orbited by large satellites known as **exoplanets**.

HAT-P-32b is 1,044 light-years from Earth and orbits a Sun-like star. Its **radius** is **twice** that of Jupiter. However, its **mass** is slightly **less** than that of Jupiter.

The exoplanet **K2-137b** was discovered in 2017. It orbits its star in less than **5 hours**—the **shortest orbit** of any known planet.

KEPLER-186F WAS THE FIRST EARTH-SIZED EXOPLANET TO BE DISCOVERED IN THE HABITABLE ZONE OF A STAR.

THE INTERNATIONAL SPACE STATION IS THE **LARGEST** HUMAN-MADE OBJECT TO ORBIT EARTH.

HOW BIG IS THE
BIGGEST STAR?

Hypergiant stars can be **hundreds of times** wider than the **Sun**. The **largest known star** is called **VY Canis Majoris**, whose diameter is nearly **1.25 billion miles** (2 billion km).

VY Canis Majoris's **diameter is about 1,400 times bigger than** the Sun's.

FAST FACTS

If it were in the center of our Solar System, VY Canis Majoris would engulf all the inner rocky planets, including Earth. It would even swallow Jupiter, so the innermost surviving planet would be Saturn! When our own Sun begins to die in 5 billion years, it will swell to become a red giant, growing beyond the present orbit of Earth.

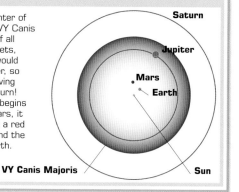

Saturn
Jupiter
Mars
Earth
VY Canis Majoris
Sun

Aldebaran is a red giant star 67 light-years away and 44 times wider than the Sun.

Arcturus is a red giant 37 light-years away and 25 times wider than the Sun. It is the fourth-brightest star in the night sky.

When compared with giant, supergiant, and hypergiant stars, our own Sun appears tiny.

Sun

H
He

IN **1925**, CECILIA PAYNE-GAPOSCHKIN DISCOVERED WHAT STARS ARE MADE OF— MOSTLY HYDROGEN AND HELIUM.

MOST **STARS** IN OUR GALAXY ARE DWARF STARS—DIM STARS ABOUT THE SIZE OF THE SUN.

SUPERNOVA

When large red giants die, their cores may collapse under their great gravity, then they may explode with incredible force. These explosions are called supernovas, and they blow a star's matter into space as a cloud of dust and gas called a nebula. This is the Crab Nebula, and it comes from a star that exploded like this in 1054 CE.

VY Canis Majoris is a red hypergiant about 4,000 light-years away. It is 1,400 times wider than the Sun but only 20–30 times heavier. Its outer layers are very thin—1,000 times thinner than Earth's atmosphere. VY Canis Majoris is burning very brightly, and the force of its burning is pushing its thin outer layers out into space.

Rigel is a blue-white supergiant 860 light-years away and around 75 times wider than the Sun. In spite of its distance from Earth, it is so luminous that it is still one of the brightest stars in our sky.

SUPERSIZED VY CANIS MAJORIS PRODUCES ABOUT 500,000 TIMES AS MUCH LIGHT AS THE SUN.

VY CANIS MAJORIS MAY HAVE ALREADY SHED ABOUT HALF OF ITS TOTAL MASS.

Neutron stars are among the most extreme places in the universe. Their temperature is more than 1.8 million °F (1 million °C), and some spin hundreds of times a second. Gravity on their surface is more than 200 billion times stronger than on Earth.

Neutron stars appear a dim blue-white color. Because they are so hot, they give off little visible light. Instead, they shine with more powerful X-rays.

FAST FACTS

A neutron star is the core of a giant star that has collapsed under its own gravity. The collapse squeezes the neutron star's matter into a minute space.

Earth Neutron star

Neutron stars shrink so much when they collapse that they pack a mass greater than the Sun into a sphere less than 19 miles (30 km) in diameter—about the size of a city. A neutron star's diameter is 425 times smaller than Earth's.

WHAT IS THE HEAVIEST STUFF IN THE UNIVERSE?

The **matter** in a **neutron star** is so dense that a piece the size of a **sugar cube** weighs the same as all the **humans** on **Earth**.

 A **NEUTRON STAR** HAS A DENSE CORE OF NEUTRONS SURROUNDED BY A SOLID IRON CRUST 0.6 MILE (1 KM) THICK.

 THE FASTEST-SPINNING NEUTRON STAR HAS BEEN RECORDED ROTATING AT A RATE OF 716 TIMES A SECOND.

PULSING STAR

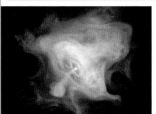

In the center of this whirling disk of hot matter is a neutron star blasting out a beam of radiation and a plume of hot gas. Thirty times every second, the beam points toward Earth, giving viewers a pulse of light.

A pinhead has a volume of ~1 cu mm. The matter in a neutron star is so dense that a pinhead-sized piece would weigh 1.1 million tons (1 million tonnes).

Pinhead-sized piece of neutron star material

A pinhead-sized blob of matter from a **neutron star** is as heavy as **three Empire State Buildings.**

The Empire State Building weighs 365,000 tons (331,000 tonnes), so three would weigh 1,095,000 tons (993,000 tonnes).

THE SOLID SURFACE OF A NEUTRON STAR IS ESTIMATED TO BE 10 BILLION TIMES STRONGER THAN STEEL.

COMPARED TO OTHER STARS, NEUTRON STARS ARE TINY— ABOUT THE SIZE OF A CITY!

HOW FAST IS
LIGHT?

It may seem to move instantly, but **light** takes time to get from place to place. In space, **light travels** at **671 million mph** (1,080,000,000 kph), or **186,282 miles** (299,792 km) in **1 second**.

Stopwatch reads
0 seconds

An imaginary light beam begins its journey.

FAST FACTS

Vacuum 100% speed

Air 99.97% speed

Water 75% speed

Glass 65% speed

Light travels at a constant speed in a vacuum, but it slows down when there are particles in the way. In air, it travels at 99.97 percent of its speed in a vacuum, in water 75 percent, and in glass about 65 percent.

This picture shows light bending, but in reality, light only curves sharply like this when pulled by really intense gravity, such as that generated by a black hole. Earth's gravity is too weak to make much difference to light's straight-line path.

1676

ASTRONOMER OLE RØMER WAS THE FIRST PERSON TO MEASURE THE SPEED OF LIGHT IN 1676.

SCIENTISTS FIRE LASER BEAMS AT MIRRORS LEFT ON THE MOON TO WORK OUT THE DISTANCE BETWEEN EARTH AND THE MOON.

In just
1 second,
a beam of light
would travel
around Earth
7.5 times.

LUNAR LASER

A laser beam traveling at the speed of light takes 1.28 seconds to reach the Moon. From this, we can precisely measure the distance from Earth to the Moon: 238,854 miles (384,399 km).

The light beam completes its 1-second journey more than 18,000 times quicker than the fastest-ever spacecraft—the New Horizons probe, which reached 36,373 mph (58,536 kph) as it left Earth's atmosphere in 2006.

00:01

Stopwatch reads 1 second

 IF YOU TRAVELED ON A PASSENGER PLANE, IT WOULD TAKE YOU **18 DAYS** TO GET TO THE MOON.

YOU CAN NEVER CATCH UP TO THE SPEED OF LIGHT— IT ALWAYS MOVES AWAY FROM YOU AT EXACTLY THE SAME SPEED!

HOW BIG IS
THE UNIVERSE?

The **universe** is **unimaginably vast**. **Distances** are so **huge** that scientists measure them in **light-years**—the distance that light travels in one year.

The **Milky Way**, a disk-shaped spiral galaxy, contains the Solar System. This galaxy is about 100,000 light-years across. One light-year is 5,879 billion miles (9,461 billion km).

FAST FACTS

ONE YEAR
J F M A
M J J A
S O N D
31

The **universe** is 13.7 billion years old. Humans have not been around for that long. If the universe were just a year old, *Homo sapiens* (humans) would only have emerged at 11:52 P.M. on New Year's Eve.

The Sun is about 93 million miles (150 million km) from planet Earth.

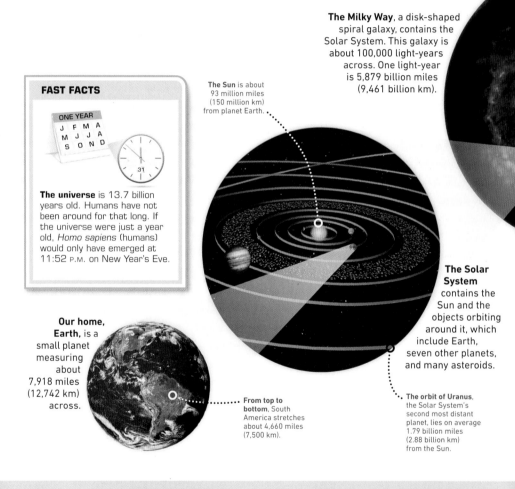

The Solar System contains the Sun and the objects orbiting around it, which include Earth, seven other planets, and many asteroids.

Our home, Earth, is a small planet measuring about 7,918 miles (12,742 km) across.

From top to bottom, South America stretches about 4,660 miles (7,500 km).

The orbit of Uranus, the Solar System's second most distant planet, lies on average 1.79 billion miles (2.88 billion km) from the Sun.

THE **UNIVERSE** INCREASED IN SIZE BY BILLIONS OF MILES (KM) IN THE SAME AMOUNT OF TIME IT TOOK YOU TO BLINK!

THE **TEMPERATURE** OF THE UNIVERSE IS ABOUT –454°F (–270°C). HOWEVER, IT'S DECREASING AS THE UNIVERSE EXPANDS.

MILKY WAY

Although disk-shaped, the Milky Way appears in our skies as a bright band. That's because Earth (and all stars visible without a telescope) sits within the disk.

The Andromeda Galaxy is a large galaxy in the Local Group.

The Local Group of galaxies takes up an area of space that is about 10 million light-years across. The Milky Way is a tiny part of the Local Group.

A supermassive black hole is thought to sit in the middle of the Milky Way. It contains as much mass as 4 million Suns.

The edge of the observable universe is 13.7 billion light-years away.

This image, taken by the Hubble Telescope, shows galaxies up to 13.7 billion light-years away. However, the universe has expanded since light left these galaxies, so they are now even farther away.

The red dots are the most distant galaxies that we can see.

THERE ARE MORE **STARS** IN THE UNIVERSE THAN GRAINS OF SAND ON EARTH.

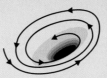

MOST OF THE **LIGHT** IN A GALAXY IS GENERATED BY MATTER SWIRLING INTO SUPERMASSIVE BLACK HOLES.

Universe data

INSIDE A STAR

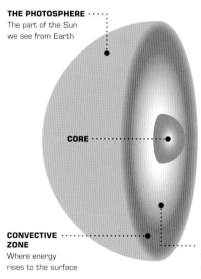

THE PHOTOSPHERE
The part of the Sun we see from Earth

CORE

CONVECTIVE ZONE
Where energy rises to the surface

RADIATIVE ZONE
Where energy shines outward in the form of light

Stars, such as our Sun, come in many different **types** and **sizes**, but all work in largely the same way. At their

cOre

atomic collisions take place that create **huge amounts of energy**. This **energy** is then **transferred** through the star to its surface and **out into space**.

OLD TIMER

13.8

The universe is believed to be 13.8 billion years old.

GALAXIES

There are four main types of galaxies:

SPIRAL

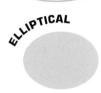
ELLIPTICAL

LENTICULAR

IRREGULAR

STAR LIFE

How a star **ends its life** depends on its size and mass. When an average Sun-like star begins to run out of fuel, it e**xpands**

AVERAGE SUN-LIKE STAR — **RED GIANT** — **PLANETARY NEBULA**

MASSIVE STAR — **RED SUPERGIANT** — **SUPERNOVA**

to become a cooler, fainter star known as a **red giant**. It eventually sheds its outer layers, forming a cloud of material called a **planetary nebula**. More massive stars become **red supergiants**, which eventually tear themselves apart in gigantic explosions known as **supernovas**.

THE UNIVERSE BEGAN 13.8 BILLION YEARS AGO WITH AN EXPLOSION—AN EVENT KNOWN AS **THE BIG BANG**.

WHEN YOU LOOK AT THE **STARS**, YOU ARE STARING INTO THE PAST—IT TAKES A LONG TIME FOR STARLIGHT TO REACH EARTH!

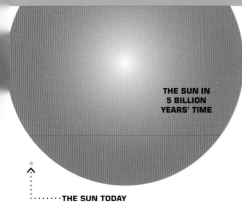

THE SUN IN 5 BILLION YEARS' TIME

THE SUN TODAY

BIG **SUNS** AND BIG
BANGS

When the **Sun dies**, in around **5 billion years'** time, it will expand to around 100 times its current width.

The most **massive** stars burn ferociously quickly and die out in just a few million years. But smaller stars, known as **red dwarfs**, can glow weakly for trillions of years. The massive star **Eta Carinae**, located 8,000 light-years from Earth, is due to **explode** as a supernova soon. When it does, it could be the

brightest

object in the sky after the Sun—bright enough to read by at night.

MILKY
WAY

Our galaxy, the **Milky Way**, is a spiral galaxy around **100,000 light-years** across. It is believed to contain more than 200 billion stars.

The nearest major galaxy to us, the **Andromeda Galaxy**, is about 2.5 million light-years away. It is **260,000 light-years across**—more than twice the size of the Milky Way— and contains around **400 billion stars**.

TRAVELING AT
LIGHT SPEED

The **speed of light** is the fastest speed there is—**186,282 miles per second** (299,792 km per second). But the universe is so vast that, even traveling at this great speed, it can take a long time to travel around.

EARTH

MOON	**1.3** SECONDS	
MARS	**4** MINUTES	
JUPITER	**35** MINUTES	
NEPTUNE	**4** HOURS	
VOYAGER	**22** HOURS	
ALPHA CENTAURI (NEAREST STAR SYSTEM)	**4** YEARS	
ANDROMEDA (NEAREST MAJOR GALAXY)	**2.5** MILLION YEARS	

SECONDS

MINUTES

HOURS

YEARS

LIGHT–SPEED TRAVEL LINE

EDGE OF UNIVERSE

45.7 BILLION YEARS

 THE MILKY WAY IS SO VAST, IT WOULD TAKE THE SUN ABOUT 230 MILLION YEARS TO COMPLETE AN ORBIT AROUND OUR GALAXY.

 WE CAN ONLY OBSERVE 5% OF THE UNIVERSE. THE REST IS DARK MATTER AND DARK ENERGY.

Astounding Earth

Since our planet formed, it has been shaped by colossal forces—from the weather to volcanic eruptions and asteroid impacts. Today, high mountains stretch skyward, canyons and caves plunge into Earth's depths, and vast rivers snake across the land.

Tourists at the Grand Canyon in Arizona marvel at the view—and the hair-raising drop! The canyon is just over 1 mile (1.6 km) deep—nearly the height of four Empire State Buildings stacked one on top of the other.

HOW BIG IS THE
LARGEST LAKE?

The water in **all five** of the North American Great Lakes combined would not fill Lake Baikal.

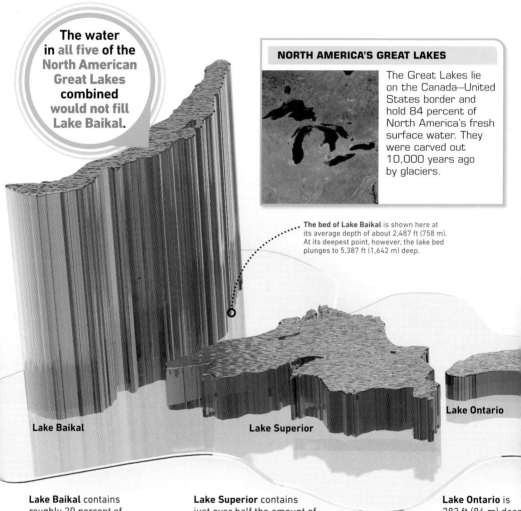

NORTH AMERICA'S GREAT LAKES

The Great Lakes lie on the Canada–United States border and hold 84 percent of North America's fresh surface water. They were carved out 10,000 years ago by glaciers.

The bed of Lake Baikal is shown here at its average depth of about 2,487 ft (758 m). At its deepest point, however, the lake bed plunges to 5,387 ft (1,642 m) deep.

Lake Baikal

Lake Superior

Lake Ontario

Lake Baikal contains roughly 20 percent of the world's unfrozen fresh surface water.

Lake Superior contains just over half the amount of water of Lake Baikal and is on average 482 ft (147 m) deep. It is the largest of the Great Lakes in terms of area, depth, and volume of water.

Lake Ontario is 282 ft (86 m) deep on average, and Lake Baikal would fill it 15 times.

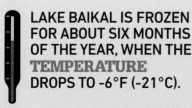

LAKE BAIKAL IS FROZEN FOR ABOUT SIX MONTHS OF THE YEAR, WHEN THE TEMPERATURE DROPS TO -6°F (-21°C).

IN WINTER, THE LAKE IS A WINTER WONDERLAND WITH HORSE-DRAWN SLEIGHS, DOG SLEDDING, AND HOVERCRAFTS.

The **largest freshwater lake** in the world by volume is **Lake Baikal** in Siberia. It contains around **6,238,500 billion gallons** (23,615,000 billion liters) of water.

FAST FACTS

The Caspian Sea, between Asia and Europe, is about 12 times larger than Lake Baikal in area and contains three times as much water. It is salty and is all that remains of an ancient ocean. Experts think of it as an inland sea rather than a lake.

Lake Baikal
The Caspian Sea

Lake Superior
Ligeia Mare
Lake Michigan
Lake Huron

Saturn's moon Titan has several huge lakes made of liquid methane. Ligeia Mare is similar in size to one of the Great Lakes. Kraken Mare is even bigger, at around the size of the Caspian Sea.

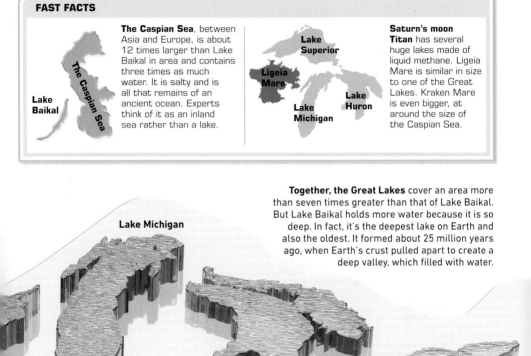

Lake Michigan

Lake Huron

Lake Erie

Together, the Great Lakes cover an area more than seven times greater than that of Lake Baikal. But Lake Baikal holds more water because it is so deep. In fact, it's the deepest lake on Earth and also the oldest. It formed about 25 million years ago, when Earth's crust pulled apart to create a deep valley, which filled with water.

Lake Michigan has an average depth of 279 ft (85 m) and contains one-fifth the amount of water in Lake Baikal.

Lake Huron has an average depth of 194 ft (59 m) and one-seventh of the amount of water in Lake Baikal.

Lake Erie is only 62 ft (19 m) deep on average. It would take nearly 50 lakes this size to fill Lake Baikal.

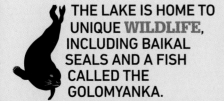

THE LAKE IS HOME TO UNIQUE WILDLIFE, INCLUDING BAIKAL SEALS AND A FISH CALLED THE GOLOMYANKA.

THE AREA AROUND THE LAKE IS KNOWN FOR ITS SIZZLING HOT SPRINGS SHOOTING THROUGH EARTH'S CRUST.

WHAT IS THE
BIGGEST RIVER?

Although not as **long** as the **Nile**, the **Amazon** carries **far more water**. It empties **58 million gallons** (219 million liters) into the ocean every second—that's **one fifth** of all the **world's river water flow**.

Along much of its length, the Amazon is 1–6 miles (1.6–10 km) wide in the dry season. However, in the rainy season, some parts expand to 30 miles (48 km) or more.

Pará River

FAST FACTS

The Amazon Basin is the area drained by the Amazon River. It is almost as big as Australia and is the largest river basin in the world. It covers 40 percent of South America, and all of it receives heavy yearly rainfall, which swells the river with water.

The Pará River joins the Amazon at its mouth, broadening its estuary even farther.

The Amazon spreads out when it reaches the Atlantic Ocean and merges with the mouth of another wide river, the Pará. This image shows the region around this mouth, or estuary—sometimes called "The Mouths of the Amazon."

THE AMAZON IS HOME TO 10% OF ALL KNOWN **CREATURES** IN THE WORLD.

ON AVERAGE, A NEW SPECIES OF **PLANT** OR **ANIMAL** IS FOUND IN THE AMAZON RAINFOREST EVERY OTHER DAY.

More than 1,100 tributaries feed directly into the Amazon, more than 15 of which are themselves over 620 miles (1,000 km) long.

FLOODED RAINFOREST

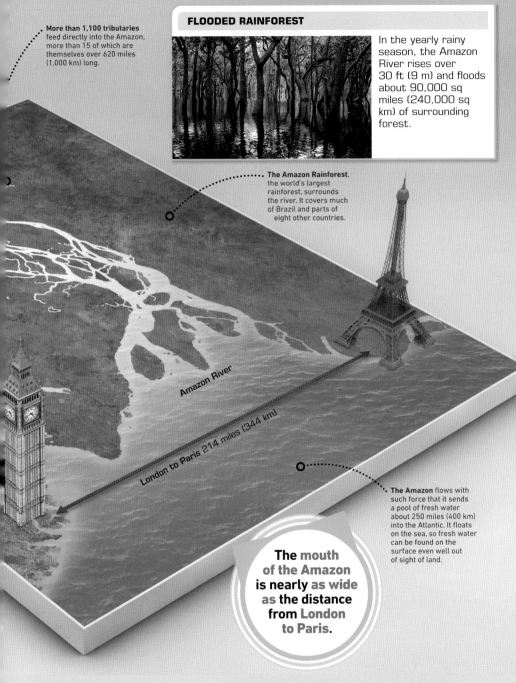

In the yearly rainy season, the Amazon River rises over 30 ft (9 m) and floods about 90,000 sq miles (240,000 sq km) of surrounding forest.

The Amazon Rainforest, the world's largest rainforest, surrounds the river. It covers much of Brazil and parts of eight other countries.

Amazon River

London to Paris 214 miles (344 km)

The Amazon flows with such force that it sends a pool of fresh water about 250 miles (400 km) into the Atlantic. It floats on the sea, so fresh water can be found on the surface even well out of sight of land.

The mouth of the Amazon is nearly as wide as the distance from London to Paris.

THE AMAZON HOLDS **20%** OF THE WORLD'S FLOWING FRESH WATER.

THERE ARE **NO BRIDGES** ACROSS THE AMAZON RIVER, SO IT IS ONLY PASSABLE BY BOAT OR SWIMMING!

HOW HIGH IS THE TALLEST
WATERFALL?

The **tallest waterfall** in the world, **Angel Falls** in Venezuela, is **3,212 ft (979 m) in height**. Known locally as **Kerepakupai Merú**, it found fame when US pilot **Jimmy Angel** flew over the waterfall in 1933.

Vinnufossen, Norway
2,837 ft (865 m)

Sutherland Falls, New Zealand
1,903 ft (580 m)

Angel Falls is formed by water tumbling down the side of one of the tepuis, Venezuela's vertical-sided mountains. Here, it is pictured next to some of the world's other tall and famous waterfalls.

VICTORIA FALLS

Victoria Falls forms the largest continuous sheet of falling water in the world, at 1.1 mile (1.7 km) wide and 354 ft (108 m) tall.

Sutherland Falls drops down the almost sheer side of a fjord—a valley carved by a glacier and flooded by the sea.

Victoria Falls, Zambia/Zimbabwe
354 ft (108 m)

Niagara Falls, US/Canada
187 ft (57 m)

The spray can be seen from 30 miles (48 km) away.

ANGEL FALLS DROPS DOWN FROM THE GAUJA RIVER, WHICH LATVIAN EXPLORER **ALEKSANDRS LAIME** NAMED AFTER A RIVER IN HIS HOME COUNTRY.

THE **STEEP DROP** OF ANGEL FALLS TURNS MOST WATER FROM THE GAUJA RIVER TO MIST BEFORE IT REACHES THE BOTTOM.

Angel Falls, Venezuela
3,212 ft (979 m)

FAST FACTS

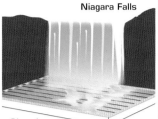

Niagara Falls

Olympic swimming pool

Niagara Falls has the highest water flow rate of any waterfall in North America. In just 1 second, 740,000 gallons (2.8 million liters) of water gushes over the falls—enough to fill an Olympic swimming pool.

In 1901, Ann Taylor became the first person to go over Niagara Falls in a barrel and survive to tell the tale. Of the 14 other people who have intentionally gone over the falls since, five did not survive the experience.

The Empire State Building measures 1,453 ft (443 m) tall.

Angel Falls is more than twice as tall as New York's Empire State Building.

IN 2019, PAWEL JANKOWSKI BASE JUMPED FROM THE TOP OF ANGEL FALLS AND RECORDED HIS FREE FALL!

THE SURROUNDING CANAIMA NATIONAL PARK IS HOME TO INCREDIBLE WILDLIFE, INCLUDING JAGUARS AND GIANT ANTEATERS.

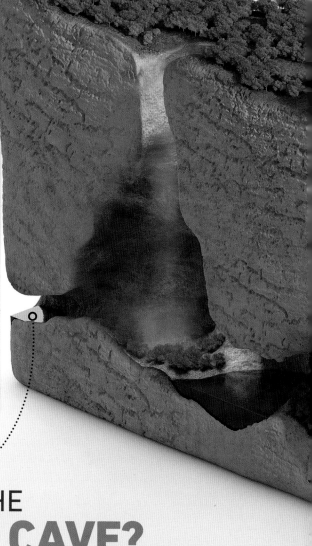

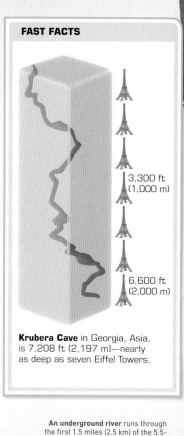
An underground river runs through
the first 1.5 miles (2.5 km) of the 5.5-
mile (9-km) cave. There are thought to
be more than 150 chambers in total.

HOW BIG IS THE
BIGGEST CAVE?

Deep in the **Vietnamese jungle** lies the **Hang
Son Doong** cave—the **biggest** in the **world**.
In places, it is more than **650 ft** (200 m) **high**.

IN 1991, LOCAL FARMER
HO KHANH WAS
SEEKING SHELTER FROM
A STORM WHEN HE CAME
ACROSS THE GAPING
ENTRANCE TO THE CAVE.

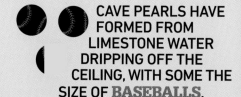

CAVE PEARLS HAVE
FORMED FROM
LIMESTONE WATER
DRIPPING OFF THE
CEILING, WITH SOME THE
SIZE OF **BASEBALLS**.

Each of the sinkholes on the surface is up to 330 ft (100 m) across.

The **Hang Son Doong** cave was not discovered until 1991 because it was hidden by thick jungle. The cave formed between 2 and 5 million years ago as underground river water eroded the limestone rock. In places where the rock was weak, the ceiling collapsed into giant sinkholes.

Six Towers of Pisa would fit in the deepest shaft if stacked on top of one another.

ROCK PILLARS

Stalagmites in the cave, like the "Hand of Dog" shown here, are so big that they make the man standing in the middle look tiny.

The two main chambers within the cave system have 100-ft (30-m) trees growing inside because the roofs fell in and let in enough light for plants to grow.

THE TREES INSIDE THE CAVE PROVIDE A HOME FOR MANY ANIMALS, INCLUDING FLYING FOXES.

ROCKS IN THE CAVE CONTAIN FOSSILIZED CORALS AND SEA LILIES THAT ARE 300 MILLION YEARS OLD.

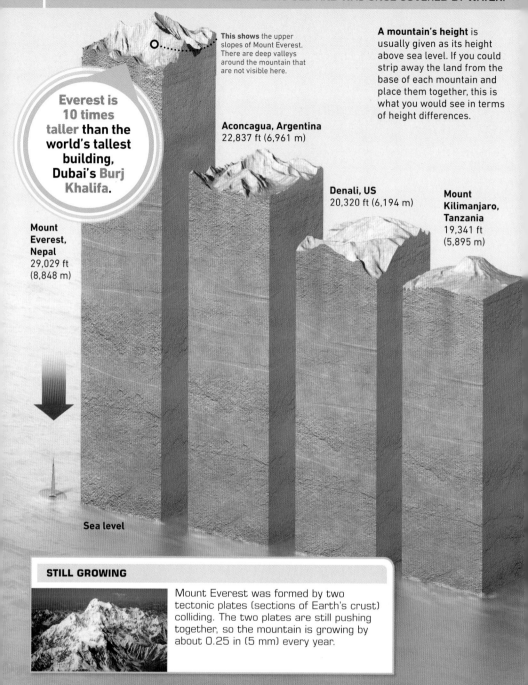

This shows the upper slopes of Mount Everest. There are deep valleys around the mountain that are not visible here.

A mountain's height is usually given as its height above sea level. If you could strip away the land from the base of each mountain and place them together, this is what you would see in terms of height differences.

Everest is **10 times taller** than the world's tallest building, Dubai's **Burj Khalifa**.

Aconcagua, Argentina
22,837 ft (6,961 m)

Denali, US
20,320 ft (6,194 m)

Mount Kilimanjaro, Tanzania
19,341 ft (5,895 m)

Mount Everest, Nepal
29,029 ft (8,848 m)

Sea level

STILL GROWING

Mount Everest was formed by two tectonic plates (sections of Earth's crust) colliding. The two plates are still pushing together, so the mountain is growing by about 0.25 in (5 mm) every year.

IN 1953, **EDMUND HILLARY** AND **TENZING NORGAY** BECAME THE FIRST TO REACH THE SUMMIT OF EVEREST.

MOUNT EVEREST IS THE ULTIMATE DANGER ZONE— CLIMBERS FACE FALLING ROCKS, AVALANCHES, REDUCED OXYGEN, AND ALTITUDE SICKNESS.

HOW HIGH IS
MOUNT EVEREST?

The peak of **Mount Everest**, the **highest mountain** in the world, is **29,029 ft (8,848 m)** above sea level.

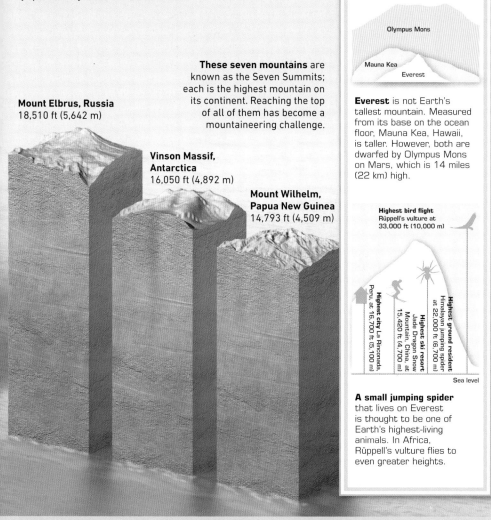

These seven mountains are known as the Seven Summits; each is the highest mountain on its continent. Reaching the top of all of them has become a mountaineering challenge.

Mount Elbrus, Russia
18,510 ft (5,642 m)

Vinson Massif, Antarctica
16,050 ft (4,892 m)

Mount Wilhelm, Papua New Guinea
14,793 ft (4,509 m)

FAST FACTS

Olympus Mons

Mauna Kea

Everest

Everest is not Earth's tallest mountain. Measured from its base on the ocean floor, Mauna Kea, Hawaii, is taller. However, both are dwarfed by Olympus Mons on Mars, which is 14 miles (22 km) high.

Highest bird flight
Rüppell's vulture at 33,000 ft (10,000 m)

Highest ground resident
Himalayan jumping spider at 22,000 ft (6,700 m)

Highest ski resort
Jade Dragon Snow Mountain, China, at 15,420 ft (4,700 m)

Highest city La Rinconada, Peru, at 16,700 ft (5,100 m)

Sea level

A small jumping spider that lives on Everest is thought to be one of Earth's highest-living animals. In Africa, Rüppell's vulture flies to even greater heights.

THERE IS ABOUT **66%** LESS OXYGEN ON THE SUMMIT OF MOUNT EVEREST THAN AT SEA LEVEL.

THE TIBETAN NAME FOR MOUNT EVEREST IS **CHOMOLUNGMA**, WHICH MEANS "MOTHER GODDESS OF THE WORLD."

FAST FACTS

The Australian, Arabian, and Sahara deserts are hot deserts in the tropics. The biggest is the Sahara in Africa, which is as big as the US. The Kalahari and Gobi lie farther from the equator and can be cool or even very cold.

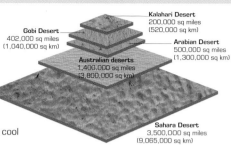

Gobi Desert
402,000 sq miles
(1,040,000 sq km)

Kalahari Desert
200,000 sq miles
(520,000 sq km)

Arabian Desert
500,000 sq miles
(1,300,000 sq km)

Australian deserts
1,400,000 sq miles
(3,800,000 sq km)

Sahara Desert
3,500,000 sq miles
(9,065,000 sq km)

The biggest erg, or sand sea, is the Rub' al Khali in the Arabian Desert. At 251,000 sq miles (650,000 sq km), it covers an area bigger than France.

France

HOW TALL ARE
SAND DUNES?

Tall dunes often reach **1,500 ft** (450 m) in height, but occasionally, dunes can even **grow** to **4,000 ft** (1,200 m).

Trains of camels were the best method of transport in the Sahara for many centuries and are still sometimes used to carry goods across the desert.

MARTIAN SAND DUNES

Near Mars's north pole is a field of dunes covered with frozen pink carbon dioxide in winter. In spring, dark sand trickles down the slopes as the carbon dioxide turns to gas.

EVERY DUNE HAS TWO SIDES: THE WINDWARD SIDE WHERE THE WIND BLOWS AND THE SMOOTH SLIP-FACE WITHOUT ANY WIND.

SANDSTORMS OCCUR WHEN WINDS IN EXCESS OF 25 MPH (40 KPH) WHIP UP SAND INTO THE AIR.

Desert

Land

Sand dunes

One third of Earth's land surface is desert, but only 10 percent of the deserts are sand dunes. The rest is rock, earth, and sheets of sand.

The peak is sculpted by winds blowing from many directions piling sand up into the center.

Saharan trader with camel loaded with goods

You could bury the Eiffel Tower inside a big Saharan star dune.

This Saharan star dune is 1,500 ft (450 m) tall. Star dunes are pyramid-shaped and tend to form in areas without a dominant wind direction.

Dust devils are columns of dusty air heated by the Sun. They begin to spin as they rise through the cooler air above.

Great Pyramid Original height 481 ft (147 m)

Eiffel Tower 1,083 ft (330 m)

THE SANDFISH IS A SMALL LIZARD THAT DRAWS BACK ITS LEGS TO "SWIM" THROUGH THE SAHARA SANDS.

CAMELS ARE KNOWN AS "SHIPS OF THE DESERT" BECAUSE THEY CAN CARRY HEAVY LOADS LONG DISTANCES.

HOW POWERFUL WAS THE
KRAKATOA VOLCANO?

In **1883**, Krakatoa, a volcano in **Indonesia**, erupted with a force of about **200 megatons** of **TNT** explosive or **several nuclear bombs**.

Krakatoa produced one of the greatest volcanic eruptions in history. It destroyed more than two-thirds of Krakatoa island, killing more than 36,000 people. People reported hearing the explosion 2,800 miles (4,500 km) away.

ASH CLOUD LIGHTNING

The electrical charge in the ash cloud from a volcanic eruption can cause lightning, as in the 2010 Eyjafjallajökull eruption in Iceland.

THE KRAKATOA ERUPTION TRIGGERED GIANT TSUNAMI WAVES MEASURING ABOUT 120 FT (37 M) IN HEIGHT.

ABOUT 165 VILLAGES AND TOWNS NEAR KRAKATOA WERE DESTROYED BY THE TSUNAMI.

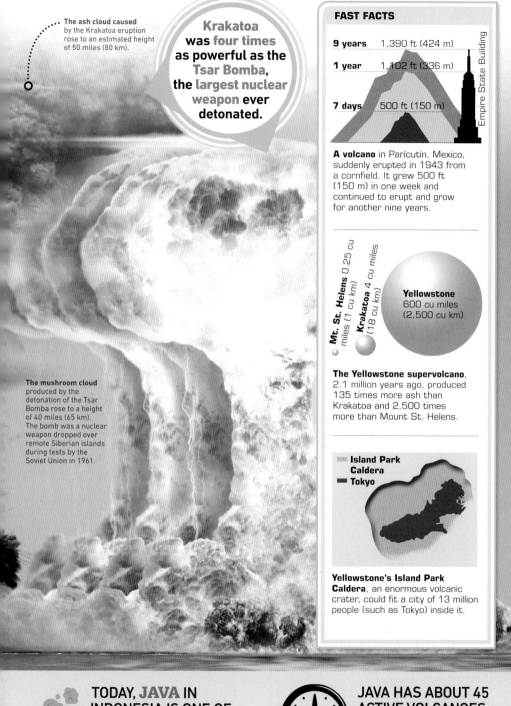

The ash cloud caused by the Krakatoa eruption rose to an estimated height of 50 miles (80 km).

Krakatoa **was four times as powerful as the Tsar Bomba,** the largest nuclear **weapon** ever detonated.

The mushroom cloud produced by the detonation of the Tsar Bomba rose to a height of 40 miles (65 km). The bomb was a nuclear weapon dropped over remote Siberian islands during tests by the Soviet Union in 1961.

FAST FACTS

9 years	1,390 ft (424 m)
1 year	1,102 ft (336 m)
7 days	500 ft (150 m)

Empire State Building

A volcano in Parícutin, Mexico, suddenly erupted in 1943 from a cornfield. It grew 500 ft (150 m) in one week and continued to erupt and grow for another nine years.

Mt. St. Helens 0.25 cu miles (1 cu km)

Krakatoa 4 cu miles (18 cu km)

Yellowstone 600 cu miles (2,500 cu km)

The Yellowstone supervolcano, 2.1 million years ago, produced 135 times more ash than Krakatoa and 2,500 times more than Mount St. Helens.

Island Park Caldera
Tokyo

Yellowstone's Island Park Caldera, an enormous volcanic crater, could fit a city of 13 million people (such as Tokyo) inside it.

TODAY, JAVA IN INDONESIA IS ONE OF THE MOST VOLCANIC AREAS ON EARTH— KRAKATOA ERUPTED CLOSE TO JAVA.

JAVA HAS ABOUT 45 ACTIVE VOLCANOES— SEMERU, JAVA'S HIGHEST VOLCANO, ERUPTS EVERY 10–30 MINUTES.

WHAT'S THE LARGEST
CRATER ON EARTH?

Asteroid and **comet** impacts make **craters** on **Earth** just like on the Moon. The **largest** one is the **Vredefort crater** in South Africa, which is over **186 miles** (300 km) **wide**.

You could fit **250 Barringer craters into four Vredefort craters.**

Barringer crater is a well-preserved impact crater in Arizona. Its shape is so clear because it is only 50,000 years old.

Asteroids and comets have battered Earth over the course of its life, but we can see only a few clear craters on Earth's surface today. This is because most craters are worn down or buried under younger rock.

THE VREDEFORT **IMPACT** DID NOT CAUSE A MASS EXTINCTION—THERE WERE ONLY BASIC LIFEFORMS AT THAT TIME.

DUST CLOUDS FROM THE IMPACT WOULD HAVE COMPLETELY BLOCKED OUT **THE SUN.**

FAST FACTS

Herschel crater central peak
21,300 ft
(6,500 m)

Mt. Everest
29,029 ft
(8,848 m)

Saturn's moon Mimas is marked by a huge crater named Herschel with a central peak made by the shockwave of an impact. The peak is nearly as tall as Mount Everest.

The Borealis Basin on Mars is thought to be the biggest known land feature caused by an impact. If it is, it must have been the result of a blow from an object the size of Pluto. The basin covers most of the northern half of Mars and is nearly five times the size of the US.

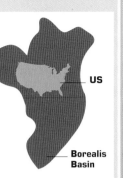

US

Borealis Basin

Barringer crater is only ¾ mile (1.2 km) in diameter.

Chicxulub crater in Mexico is 110 miles (180 km) wide. It was formed about 66 million years ago by the impact of an object 6 miles (10 km) across hitting Earth. The destruction it caused is thought to have wiped out the dinosaurs. The crater is now buried and half of it is hidden on the seabed.

Vredefort crater was made around 2 billion years ago. In all that time, it has been eroded by wind, rain, and rivers and bent and distorted by movements in the Earth's crust.

BIGGEST METEORITE

When an object falls from space and survives the impact, it is known as a meteorite. The Hoba meteorite in Namibia is the biggest ever found and weighs more than 60 tons (66 tonnes).

PREHISTORIC **ROCK CARVINGS** DISCOVERED IN THE CRATER DEPICT ANTELOPES, HIPPOS, AND RHINOS.

THE CRATER AREA IS A **HABITAT** FOR AT LEAST 200 TYPES OF BIRDS AS WELL AS OTHER ANIMALS.

HOW BIG ARE THE BIGGEST
CRYSTALS?

Crystals of **selenite** discovered in a cave in **Mexico** measure up to **37.4 ft (11.4 m) long**.

With temperatures in the cave of 118°F (48°C) and 98 percent humidity, people have to wear protective suits to explore the amazing crystal formations.

FAST FACTS

The longest Naica crystal found so far, Crystal Cin, is around the length of a bus and weighs about the same as 8 African elephants!

Crystal Cin

Length 37.4 ft (11.4 m)

Single-decker bus

The oldest crystal in the cave dates back 600,000 years—about the time when *Homo heidelbergensis*, the ancestors of modern humans, first appeared.

Present day

600,000 years ago

 IN 2000, TWO MINING BROTHERS DRILLED A TUNNEL UNDER NAICA, ONLY TO DISCOVER THIS GAPING CAVERN FULL OF **CRYSTALS**.

 THIS CAVE IS SWELTERINGLY HOT BECAUSE IT IS SITUATED OVER A HOT **MAGMA CHAMBER** INSIDE EARTH.

These vast selenite crystals are in the Cave of Crystals, which lies 985 ft (300 m) below ground in a mine at Naica, northern Mexico. When the caves were flooded with groundwater rich in calcium sulfate, selenite crystals grew slowly until the mines were drained of water.

FINGAL'S CAVE

Fingal's Cave off the coast of Scotland is unique. It is formed from hexagonal pillars of basalt rock more than 65 ft (20 m) tall. They formed when an ancient lava flow cooled and cracked.

The largest crystals in the cave are more than six times taller than a person.

THE BIGGEST OF THE CAVE'S CRYSTALS WEIGHS A STAGGERING 60 TONS (55 TONNES)— THE SAME AS NINE ELEPHANTS.

IN 2017, SCIENTISTS DISCOVERED MICROBES INSIDE THE CRYSTALS— THEY WERE ABOUT 50,000 YEARS OLD.

HOW MUCH WATER
IS THERE?

The world contains **332 million cu miles** (1.3 billion cu km) of **water** in its oceans, rivers, lakes, groundwater, and clouds and—as **ice**—in its glaciers and ice caps.

Scooped up, the world's water would form a ball 860 miles (1,384 km) wide.

ICE CAPS AND GLACIERS

Only 2.5 percent of the world's water is fresh, and most of this fresh water is locked up in glaciers and ice caps. This leaves less than 1 percent of Earth's water that is liquid and fresh.

This globe shows the ocean basins with all their water removed. Nearly 97 percent of the world's water is in oceans. The next biggest store of water is the ice caps and glaciers, with 1.75 percent.

AS WELL AS THE LARGEST, **THE PACIFIC** IS THE WORLD'S OLDEST AND DEEPEST OCEAN.

AS THE TECTONIC PLATES SLOWLY MOVE APART EVERY YEAR, THE **ATLANTIC** WIDENS BY ABOUT 1.6 IN (4 CM).

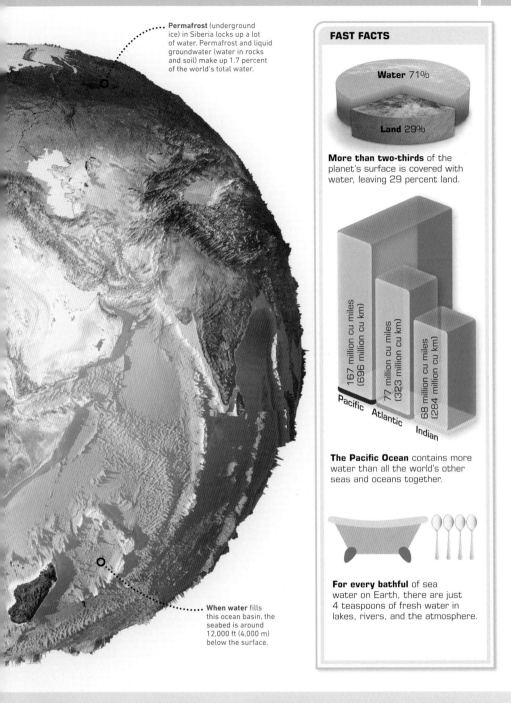

Permafrost (underground ice) in Siberia locks up a lot of water. Permafrost and liquid groundwater (water in rocks and soil) make up 1.7 percent of the world's total water.

When water fills this ocean basin, the seabed is around 12,000 ft (4,000 m) below the surface.

FAST FACTS

Water 71%

Land 29%

More than two-thirds of the planet's surface is covered with water, leaving 29 percent land.

167 million cu miles (696 million cu km)

77 million cu miles (323 million cu km)

68 million cu miles (284 million cu km)

Pacific   Atlantic   Indian

The Pacific Ocean contains more water than all the world's other seas and oceans together.

For every bathful of sea water on Earth, there are just 4 teaspoons of fresh water in lakes, rivers, and the atmosphere.

IF YOU DROPPED A STONE IN THE **DEEPEST** PART OF THE OCEAN, IT WOULD TAKE OVER AN HOUR TO HIT THE BOTTOM.

THE OCEANS ARE DIVIDED INTO **FIVE ZONES**, FROM THE SUNLIGHT ZONE ON THE SURFACE TO THE HADAL ZONE IN THE DEEPEST DEPTHS.

HOW DEEP IS
THE OCEAN?

Continental shelves are the shallow regions fringing deep oceans. They are actually part of the continental landmass. A shelf may extend hundreds of miles (km) from the coast. ....

The **average depth** of the ocean is 12,080 ft (3,682 m), but the **deepest point** is **36,188 ft** (11,030 m) below sea level at **Challenger Deep** in the Pacific Ocean.

It would take **29 stacked Empire State Buildings** to reach the bottom of Challenger Deep.

BARRELEYE

This barreleye, or spookfish, is one of the many peculiar creatures that inhabit the dark ocean depths. The barreleye lives 2,000–2,600 ft (600–800 m) under water and has unique tube-shaped eyes inside a transparent head.

The Empire State Building measures 1,250 ft (381 m) to the top of its roof.

TINY AMPHIPODS LIVE IN THE OCEAN DEPTHS—THEIR SOFT BODIES ENABLE THEM TO SURVIVE THE BONE-CRUSHING WATER PRESSURE.

THE DEEPEST FISH IN THE OCEAN IS A SNAILFISH DISCOVERED IN 2023 IN A MARINE TRENCH NEAR JAPAN.

Continental shelf
Shoreline to 460 ft (140 m)

Continental slope
460–10,500 ft
(140–3,200 m)

Abyssal plain
10,500–20,000 ft
(3,200–6,000 m)

Ocean trench
20,000–36,200 ft
(6,000–11,030 m)

Challenger Deep
36,200 ft (11,030 m)

The seabed is not flat. It starts with a gradual descent down the continental shelf where the land gives way to the sea along the coast. It then plunges down the continental slope to the deep ocean floor, or abyssal plain. The seabed has ridges or deep trenches, such as the Mariana Trench, where Challenger Deep is located.

FAST FACTS

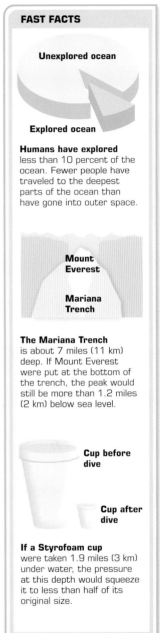

Unexplored ocean

Explored ocean

Humans have explored less than 10 percent of the ocean. Fewer people have traveled to the deepest parts of the ocean than have gone into outer space.

Mount Everest

Mariana Trench

The Mariana Trench is about 7 miles (11 km) deep. If Mount Everest were put at the bottom of the trench, the peak would still be more than 1.2 miles (2 km) below sea level.

Cup before dive

Cup after dive

If a Styrofoam cup were taken 1.9 miles (3 km) under water, the pressure at this depth would squeeze it to less than half of its original size.

IN 1960, A CREW OF TWO PEOPLE WERE THE FIRST TO VISIT THE MARIANA TRENCH ABOARD THE SUBMERSIBLE *TRIESTE*.

IN 2012, FILMMAKER JAMES CAMERON BECAME THE FIRST SOLO EXPLORER TO REACH CHALLENGER DEEP, TAKING 2 HOURS AND 36 MINUTES.

HOW TALL WAS
THE BIGGEST
WAVE EVER SURFED?

In 2020, German professional big-wave surfer **Sebastian Steudtner** surfed a **wave** that was **86 ft** (26.2 m) **tall** off the coast of Nazaré, Portugal.

Record waves occur off Nazaré because it faces the huge swells caused by distant Atlantic storms. An undersea canyon then funnels the wave energy of the swells onto a short stretch of the coast, piling the waters high.

FAST FACTS

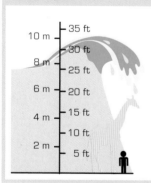

10 m — 35 ft
— 30 ft
8 m — 25 ft
6 m — 20 ft
4 m — 15 ft
— 10 ft
2 m — 5 ft

Tsunamis tend to be less than 33 ft (10 m) tall, but because there is a lot of water following behind them, they cause a flood that reaches far inland. They are caused by earthquakes on the seabed, land slips, and asteroid strikes.

Highest tsunami
1,720 ft (520 m)

Highest ocean waves 115 ft (35 m)

Highest surfed wave 86 ft (26.2 m)

The biggest wave ever known occurred in Lituya Bay, Alaska, when a slab of rock slipped into the bay and caused a huge tsunami. Giant ocean waves also form far out at sea, caused by high winds and strong currents.

IN 1778, CAPTAIN JAMES COOK WAS AMAZED TO SEE SURFERS IN TAHITI AND DOCUMENTED THE DISCOVERY IN HIS DIARY.

THE WORLD'S BEST BIG-WAVE SURFERS COME TO NAZARÉ IN THE HOPE OF CATCHING THE ELUSIVE 100-FT (30-M) WAVE.

Foaming breakers rise up almost vertically before curling over to form a tube. The surfer tries to stay inside the tube and, if possible, reach the end of it before the wave collapses.

An **86-ft (26.2-m) wave is** the **height** of more than **14 people** standing on top of each other.

Surfboards come in a variety of sizes. This championship board is 7 ft (2.1 m) long.

TSUNAMI DAMAGE

Tsunamis are so powerful that anything in their way is flattened and swept away. Even large ships can be carried inland, leaving them stranded miles from the shore.

ENGINEERS NOW DESIGN UNDERWATER MACHINES TO GENERATE PERFECT **OCEAN WAVES** FOR SURFERS TO RIDE.

AMERICAN SURFING DOG RICOCHET COMPETED IN ABOUT 20 SURFING COMPETITIONS AND WON **NINE GOLD MEDALS**.

HOW BIG WAS THE
BIGGEST ICEBERG?

The **biggest-ever** iceberg began its life when it broke free from an ice shelf off **Antarctica** in 1956. It was **208 miles** (335 km) **long** and **62 miles** (100 km) **wide**.

Antwerp

Brussels

Ghent

Bruges

B E L G

Flanders

The biggest iceberg was not really shaped like Belgium. It was longer and thinner, but its area of 12,000 sq miles (31,000 sq km) was slightly larger than Belgium's. It was even larger than iceberg B-15—the Jamaica-sized iceberg that broke off Antarctica's Ross Ice Shelf in 2000.

HIDDEN DEPTHS

Icebergs float low in the water, with around 90 percent of their height hidden beneath the waves. The ice below the water melts faster than that above it, so an iceberg may suddenly roll over with a great crash that can be heard for miles.

CALVING IS THE PROCESS BY WHICH ICEBERGS BREAK AWAY FROM GLACIERS AND VAST ICE SHEETS.

THE *TITANIC* SANK ON ITS MAIDEN VOYAGE IN 1912 AFTER HITTING AN ICEBERG IN THE ATLANTIC.

The **biggest-ever iceberg** covered an area **larger than that** of Belgium.

Belgium covers an area of 11,787 sq miles (30,528 sq km), which is about the same as Maryland.

Liege

I U M

Charleroi

Ardennes

The height of the iceberg is exaggerated in this picture. It would have stood no more than 500 ft (150 m) above the sea surface.

FAST FACTS

Glaciers

Snail

Glaciers are rivers of ice that move very slowly, averaging only 12 in (30 cm) a day. A fast snail can zip across this distance in 2¼ minutes.

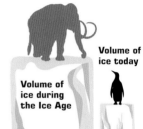

Volume of ice today

Volume of ice during the Ice Age

In the last ice age, ice covered more than 30 percent of the planet. Nearly 60 percent of it has melted since then, leaving us with ice only in mountain regions and in the ice caps at the poles.

Tallest iceberg 550 ft (168 m)

Great Pyramid 482 ft (147 m)

The tallest iceberg was sighted near Greenland in 1957. Standing even higher above sea level than the Great Pyramid, the iceberg may have extended a further 4,900 ft (1,500 m) below the surface.

LARGE FRAGMENTS OF ICEBERGS ARE CALLED **BERGY BITS**, AND SMALL FRAGMENTS ARE CALLED **GROWLERS**.

TABULAR ICEBERGS HAVE STEEP SIDES AND A FLAT TOP, AND NONTABULAR ICEBERGS CAN BE **ANY SHAPE**.

WHAT IF ALL THE
ICE MELTED?

Ten percent of the **world's land** is covered by thick **glaciers** and **ice sheets**. If it all melted, the **sea level** would rise by up to **230 ft** (70 m). Many **major world cities** would be **covered** by the **ocean**.

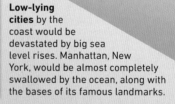

SHRINKING GLACIERS

Glaciers are great rivers of slowly flowing ice. The ice builds up over many years from fallen snow. Glaciers can begin on any high ground where the snow does not thaw completely in spring. In parts of the Arctic, glaciers reach down to the sea, but most are shrinking. Between 1941 and 2004, the Muir Glacier in Alaska (above) retreated more than 7 miles (12 km) and the sea filled its valley.

Low-lying cities by the coast would be devastated by big sea level rises. Manhattan, New York, would be almost completely swallowed by the ocean, along with the bases of its famous landmarks.

GREENLAND'S ICE SHEET IS MELTING AT A RATE OF 270 BILLION TONS (245 BILLION TONNES) A YEAR.

MELTING SEA ICE IN THE ARCTIC IS MAKING IT HARDER FOR **POLAR BEARS** TO HUNT PREY.

The first 18 floors of the Empire State Building would be flooded if the sea level rose by 230 ft (70 m).

If the **world's ice melted**, the Statue of Liberty would stand **waist-deep** in water.

FAST FACTS

Current coastline

Coastline after flooding

If all the ice melted, the coastlines of many countries would dramatically change. Britain and Ireland would turn into a group of smaller islands. Low-lying countries such as Bangladesh and the Netherlands would almost disappear.

The ice over Antarctica is extremely thick, averaging 6,000 ft (1,830 m)— nearly as deep as six Eiffel Towers. In some places, it is more than twice as deep, at 15,670 ft (4,776 m).

The Statue of Liberty's pedestal is 154 ft (47 m) high.

The base of the statue's pedestal is only about 20 ft (6 m) above current sea level.

RISING SEA LEVELS MEAN SOME LOW-LYING TROPICAL ISLANDS, LIKE THE MALDIVES, COULD DISAPPEAR.

IN THE ÖTZTAL ALPS, ITALY, MELTING ICE REVEALED THE FROZEN BODY OF A MAN THAT HAD BEEN PRESERVED FOR 5,300 YEARS.

Earth data

L O N G E S T   RIVERS

FLOW RATE

The world's **longest** river is the **Nile**, but the **Amazon** is by far the **largest**. At its mouth in the Atlantic Ocean, it **carries more water** than the next four rivers combined.

RIVER	CONTINENT	LENGTH
NILE	AFRICA	**4,145 MILES** (6,670 KM)
AMAZON	SOUTH AMERICA	**3,979 MILES** (6,404 KM)
YANGTZE	ASIA	**3,963 MILES** (6,378 KM)
MISSISSIPPI-MISSOURI	NORTH AMERICA	**3,741 MILES** (6,021 KM)
YENISEI-ANGARA	ASIA	**3,442 MILES** (5,540 KM)

CHANGING CONTINENTS

Earth's crust is divided into **giant** slabs of rock called **tectonic plates**. These plates are moving constantly but very slowly. Around **200 million years ago**, all the continents were joined into one giant landmass called **Pangea**. The movement of the tectonic plates gradually **broke the continents apart** to form the Earth we know today.

FLOW RATE IN GALLONS (LITERS) PER SECOND

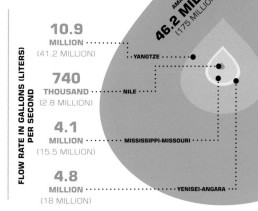

AMAZON **46.2 MILLION** (175 MILLION)

10.9 MILLION (41.2 MILLION) · · · · · · **YANGTZE** · · · · ·

740 THOUSAND (2.8 MILLION) · · · · · **NILE** · · · ·

4.1 MILLION (15.5 MILLION) · · · · **MISSISSIPPI-MISSOURI** · · · · ·

4.8 MILLION (18 MILLION) · · · · · **YENISEI-ANGARA** · · · ·

THE BIG ONES

There are **14 mountains** over 26,247 ft (**8,000 m**) high. All are found in **Asia** in the region where the Indian subcontinent is pushing into the Asian continent. In 1986, **Reinhold Messner** became the **first mountaineer to climb all 14 peaks.**

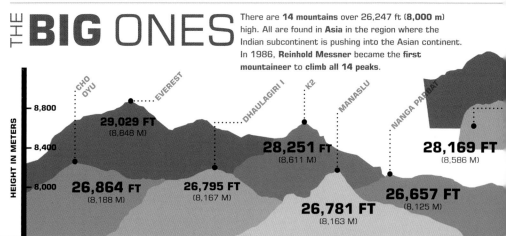

HEIGHT IN METERS

- 8,800
- 8,400
- 8,000

CHO OYU — **26,864 FT** (8,188 M)

EVEREST — **29,029 FT** (8,848 M)

DHAULAGIRI I — **26,795 FT** (8,167 M)

K2 — **28,251 FT** (8,611 M)

MANASLU — **26,781 FT** (8,163 M)

NANGA PARBAT — **28,169 FT** (8,586 M)

26,657 FT (8,125 M)

IF **EARTH'S HISTORY** WAS SQUISHED INTO ONE YEAR, PEOPLE WOULD APPEAR 25 MINUTES BEFORE MIDNIGHT ON NEW YEAR'S EVE!

EVERY YEAR, DUST FROM THE **SAHARA DESERT** BLOWS INTO THE AMAZON RAINFOREST.

INSIDE **EARTH**

Our planet is divided into several different **layers**, which get **hotter** the deeper you go. The **crust**, where we live, makes up just **0.4 percent** of Earth's mass.

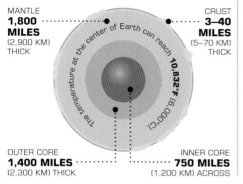

MANTLE
1,800 MILES
(2,900 KM) THICK

The temperature at the center of Earth can reach **10,832°F (6,000°C).**

CRUST
3–40 MILES
(5–70 KM) THICK

OUTER CORE
1,400 MILES
(2,300 KM) THICK

INNER CORE
750 MILES
(1,200 KM) ACROSS

MOST POWERFUL **EARTHQUAKES**

Where	When	Magnitude	Death toll
Chile	05.22.1960	9.5	4,485
Prince William Sound, Alaska	03.28.1964	9.2	128
Indian Ocean	12.26.2004	9.1	230,000
Kamchatka, Soviet Union	11.04.1952	9.0	0 (+6 cows)

5 OF THE **LARGEST** LAVA FLOWS

This image shows how much **lava** each volcanic eruption produced and how many years ago (YA) or millions of years ago (MYA) they took place.

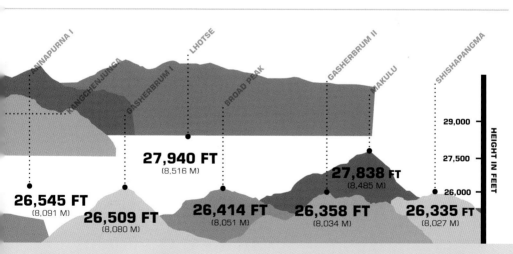

LONG VALLEY
CALIFORNIA, US
144 CU MILES
(600 CU KM),
760,000 YA

MESA FALLS
YELLOWSTONE,
US **67 CU MILES**
(280 CU KM),
1.3 MYA

LAVA CREEK
YELLOWSTONE, US
240 CU MILES
(1,000 CU KM),
640,000 YA

TOBA
SUMATRA, INDONESIA
670 CU MILES
(2,800 CU KM),
74,000 YA

HUCKLEBERRY RIDGE
YELLOWSTONE, US
590 CU MILES
(2,450 CU KM),
2.1 MYA

ANNAPURNA I

KANGCHENJUNGA

GASHERBRUM I

LHOTSE

BROAD PEAK

GASHERBRUM II

MAKALU

SHISHAPANGMA

HEIGHT IN FEET

29,000

27,500

26,000

26,545 FT
(8,091 M)

26,509 FT
(8,080 M)

27,940 FT
(8,516 M)

26,414 FT
(8,051 M)

26,358 FT
(8,034 M)

27,838 FT
(8,485 M)

26,335 FT
(8,027 M)

THE AVERAGE THICKNESS OF A TECTONIC PLATE IS 50 MILES (80 KM).

EARTH'S CRUST **MOVES** A FEW CENTIMETERS EVERY YEAR—ABOUT THE SAME RATE AS YOUR FINGERNAILS GROW.

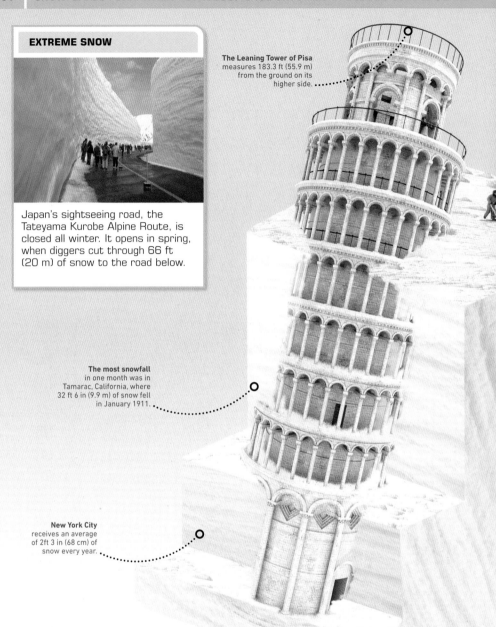

EXTREME SNOW

Japan's sightseeing road, the Tateyama Kurobe Alpine Route, is closed all winter. It opens in spring, when diggers cut through 66 ft (20 m) of snow to the road below.

The Leaning Tower of Pisa measures 183.3 ft (55.9 m) from the ground on its higher side. ·····

The most snowfall in one month was in Tamarac, California, where 32 ft 6 in (9.9 m) of snow fell in January 1911. ·····

New York City receives an average of 2ft 3 in (68 cm) of snow every year.

THE AVERAGE **SNOWFLAKE** TRAVELS AT 1.5 MPH (2.4 KPH) AND TAKES AN HOUR TO REACH THE GROUND.

SNOW ROLLERS ARE SUPER-SIZED SNOWBALLS THAT FORM AS STRONG WINDS BRING MORE SNOW TO THEIR SPHERICAL SHAPE.

WHERE IS THE SNOWIEST
PLACE ON EARTH?

The **greatest snowfall** over one year was **95 ft** (28.9 m) in **Mount Baker Ski Area**, Washington, measured in the **1998–1999** season.

FAST FACTS

Compared to snowfall records, extremes of rainfall are far higher in terms of total amount of water.

This 100-ft (30-m) pile of snow is much less dense than water. To compare it to a rainfall total, experts use a table or a mathematical equation, which would give just 8.2 ft (2.5 m) of water.

72 in (1.825 m)

Foc-Foc

The highest ever rainfall in 24 hours took place in January 1966 in Foc-Foc on the island of Réunion, where 6 ft (1.825 m) of rain fell.

Leaning Tower of Pisa 183.3 ft (55.9 m)

87 ft (26.5 m)

Cherrapunji

Cherrapunji, India, saw the most rainfall in one year in 1860–1861, when 87 ft (26.5 m) of rain fell— enough to flood almost half the Leaning Tower of Pisa.

Mount Baker's record snowfall would bury over half the Leaning Tower of Pisa.

THE LARGEST **SNOWPERSON** EVER BUILT WAS 122 FT (37 M) TALL—ALMOST AS TALL AS THE STATUE OF LIBERTY.

SNOW IS A GOOD INSULATOR, SO SOME ANIMALS, INCLUDING POLAR BEARS, MAKE SNOW DENS TO KEEP WARM.

HOW BIG WAS THE
LARGEST
HAILSTONE?

The **largest hailstone** ever known fell in **Vivian**, **South Dakota**, in a storm on **July 23, 2010**. It was **8 in (20 cm)** across.

DIVIDED IN TWO

This hailstone cut in half shows the layers of ice that form hail. Hailstones grow because winds in storm clouds throw them upward again and again. Each time, water freezes onto them, building up another layer of ice.

Giant hailstones like this form in clouds with very powerful updrafts, such as those in intense thunderstorms and tornadoes. When giant hail is finally heavy enough to fall to the ground, it can dent cars, smash windshields, flatten crops, and injure living things.

HAILSTORMS IN THE US CAUSE **DAMAGE** COSTING ABOUT $10 BILLION (£7.6 BILLION) A YEAR.

THE AREA WHERE THE **THREE US STATES** OF NEBRASKA, COLORADO, AND WYOMING MEET IS KNOWN "HAIL ALLEY."

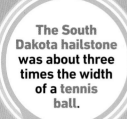

The South Dakota hailstone **was about three times the width of a tennis ball**.

FAST FACTS

Hail most often forms in giant thunderclouds, which are also the source of lightning.

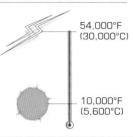

Cloud top
39,000 ft
(12,000 m)

Mount Everest
29,029 ft
(8,848 m)

Cloud base
6,600 ft (2,000 m)

Thunderclouds, technically known as cumulonimbus, are the tallest kind of clouds. They are sometimes more than 39,000 ft (12,000 m) high—half as tall again as the highest mountain. They are column-shaped with a wide, flat top.

A bolt of lightning can have a temperature of around 54,000°F (30,000°C)—more than five times hotter than the surface of the Sun, which has the hottest surface temperature of any object in the Solar System.

54,000°F (30,000°C)

10,000°F (5,600°C)

The lumps that covered the hailstone are the result of smaller hailstones colliding with each other and sticking together. Each lump is a former smaller hailstone with layers of ice added on top.

Record hailstone
8 in (20 cm) across,
1.9 lb (0.86 kg) in weight

Tennis ball
2.6 in (6.7 cm) across

WEATHER **SATELLITES** AND **RADARS** ARE USED TO DETECT THUNDERSTORMS THAT MAY PRODUCE HAILSTONES.

IN SOME COUNTRIES, COMPANIES SEND HAILSTORM **WARNINGS** TO THEIR CUSTOMERS SO THEY CAN BE PREPARED.

Weather data

HOT

The **hottest** temperature ever recorded at ground level in the shade was in **Death Valley, California**, in 1913—a scorching

134°F

(56.7°C).

AND COLD

The **coldest** temperature ever recorded at ground level was at **Vostok, Antarctica**, in 1983. It was a bone-chilling

-128.6°F (-89.2°C).

CLOUD COVER

High-level above 20,000 ft (6,000 m)

↗ CIRRUS

↙ CIRROCUMULUS

↙ CIRROSTRATUS

Midlevel 6,500–20,000 ft (2,000–6,000 m)

⫽ ALTOSTRATUS   ᴗ ALTOCUMULUS

⫽ NIMBOSTRATUS

Low-level 6,500 ft (0–2,000 m)

∿ STRATOCUMULUS   ⌒ CUMULUS   🝗 CUMULONIMBUS

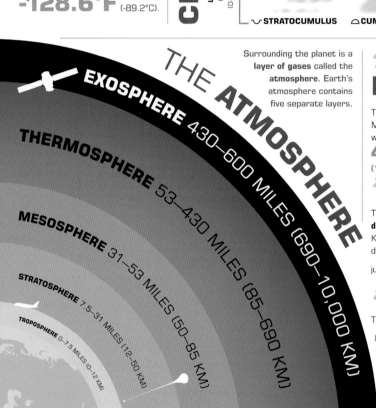

THE ATMOSPHERE

Surrounding the planet is a **layer of gases** called the **atmosphere**. Earth's atmosphere contains five separate layers.

EXOSPHERE 430–600 MILES (690–10,000 KM)

THERMOSPHERE 53–430 MILES (85–690 KM)

MESOSPHERE 31–53 MILES (50–85 KM)

STRATOSPHERE 7.5–31 MILES (12–50 KM)

TROPOSPHERE 0–7.5 MILES (0–12 KM)

RAINY DAYS

The **wettest** place on Earth is Mawsynram in northeast India, with average annual rainfall of

467 inches

(11,870 mm) per year.

The place with the **most rainy days** each year is Mt. Waialeale, Kauai, Hawaii, with **350** rainy days a year. On average, it is dry just one day a month.

The longest continuous rainfall lasted **247 days**, from August 27, 1993, to April 30, 1994, in Kaneohe Ranch, Oahu, Hawaii.

THE FIRST WEATHER **FORECAST** WAS PUBLISHED IN 1861 IN A BRITISH NEWSPAPER.

AN **ETERNAL STORM** LIGHTS UP THE SKIES OVER THE CATATUMBO RIVER IN VENEZUELA DUE TO EXCEPTIONAL STORM CLOUDS.

WINDY DAYS

The Beaufort scale lists the effects of increasing wind speeds.

BEAUFORT NUMBER	WIND SPEED	WIND EFFECT ON LAND
0	0	Smoke rises vertically
1	1–2 mph (1–3 kph)	Smoke drifts gently
2	3–7 mph (4–11 kph)	Leaves rustle
3	8–12 mph (12–19 kph)	Twigs move
4	13–18 mph (20–29 kph)	Small branches move
5	19–24 mph (30–39 kph)	Small trees sway
6	25–31 mph (40–50 kph)	Umbrellas hard to use
7	32–38 mph (51–61 kph)	Whole trees sway
8	39–46 mph (62–74 kph)	Difficulty walking
9	47–54 mph (75–87 kph)	Roofs damaged
10	55–63 mph (88–101 kph)	Trees blown down
11	64–74 mph (102–119 kph)	Houses damaged
12	over 74 mph (over 119 kph)	Buildings destroyed

TWISTERS

300 At ground level, tornadoes have the *fastest winds*. The most powerful recorded had wind speeds of mph (500 kph) or more. Tornadoes can also move at speeds of up to **70 mph** (110 kph)—far too fast for anyone to outrun.

HURRICANE DAMAGE

Hurricanes are categorized according to their speed and destructiveness using the Saffir-Simpson scale.

CATEGORY	WIND SPEED	EFFECTS	
1	**74–95 mph** (120–153 kph)	Minor building damage; branches snapped	
2	**96–110 mph** (154–177 kph)	Some roof, door, and window damage	
3	**111–130 mph** (178–208 kph)	Roof tiles dislodged; large trees uprooted	
4	**131–155 mph** (209–251 kph)	Roofs blown off; major coastal flooding	
5	**over 155 mph** (over 252 kph)	Buildings destroyed; catastrophic flooding	

FROM THE BLUE BOLTS

Lightning strikes somewhere on Earth **100** times a second. It strikes the Empire State Building roughly **25** times a year.

STRONG WINDS HAVE CARRIED ALL KINDS OF THINGS INTO THE SKY AND DROPPED THEM LIKE RAIN, INCLUDING FISH AND FROGS!

WITH 4,000 HOURS OF SUNSHINE A YEAR, THE CITY OF YUMA IN ARIZONA IS THE **SUNNIEST** PLACE ON EARTH.

WHAT WAS THE BIGGEST
NATURAL
DISASTER?

The **disease** known as the **Black Death**, which swept the world in the 14th century, **killed** up to **75 million people**.

The Rose Bowl sports stadium in Pasadena, California, has an official capacity of about 91,000 people. ·········

SPANISH FLU

In 1918, after World War I, there was a global outbreak of the disease "Spanish Flu." Spread by the mass movement of troops, it killed over 50 million people—more than the war itself. Diseases on a global scale are called pandemics.

A LARGE **CROSS** WAS PAINTED ON THE DOOR TO SHOW THAT THE PEOPLE LIVING IN THE HOUSE HAD PLAGUE.

TO **CURE** THE DISEASE, PEOPLE TRIED USING HERBAL MEDICINE OR REMOVING BLOOD FROM THE INFECTED PERSON.

The Black Death, or plague, was caused by bacteria carried by fleas on rats. It began in Asia but spread quickly as rats boarded merchant ships, taking the disease with them. The plague reached Europe in 1347, where it killed at least 30 percent of the people.

The number of **people** killed by the **Black Death** would fill **824 Rose Bowl** stadiums.

FAST FACTS

Tohoku earthquake and tsunami, Japan, 2011 $235 billion

Hurricane Katrina, US, 2005 $165 billion

Yangtze floods, China, 1998 $55 billion

Drought, US, 1988 $45 billion

The economic cost of natural disasters today can run to billions of dollars. Earthquakes can be particularly costly because they usually cause severe damage to houses and factories and key transportation links such as roads.

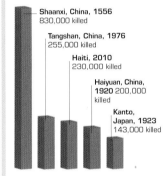

Shaanxi, China, 1556 830,000 killed

Tangshan, China, 1976 255,000 killed

Haiti, 2010 230,000 killed

Haiyuan, China, 1920 200,000 killed

Kanto, Japan, 1923 143,000 killed

Earthquakes often claim thousands of lives in built-up areas. As well as knocking down buildings, they can also cause fires due to damaged electricity cables and gas pipes.

DURING OUTBREAKS OF THE PLAGUE IN THE 17TH CENTURY, DOCTORS WORE **BEAKED MASKS** TO PROTECT THEMSELVES.

IN **1894**, KITASATO SHIBASABURŌ AND ALEXANDRE YERSIN DISCOVERED THE BACTERIA RESPONSIBLE FOR THE PLAGUE.

HOW FAST IS THE
POPULATION OF THE
WORLD GROWING?

Around **367,000 babies** are **born each day** and about **166,000 people die**. So overall, the world's population **grows by 201,000 people** every **day** of the year.

This crowd of **8,000 people** shows how much **Earth's** population increases **every single hour**.

At least another two people would be added to the crowd every second.

AGING WORLD

The world's population is getting older. Better healthcare means that more babies are surviving, so people are having fewer children. It also enables older people to live longer.

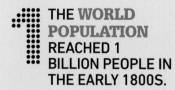

THE **WORLD POPULATION** REACHED 1 BILLION PEOPLE IN THE EARLY 1800S.

THE WORLD'S SMALLEST COUNTRY, VATICAN CITY IN ROME, HAS THE SMALLEST POPULATION, WITH ABOUT **500 INHABITANTS**.

FAST FACTS

The human population is growing faster in some places than in others. Using a graph called a population pyramid, we can see which countries have fast-growing populations.

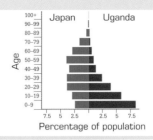

Japan | Uganda

Age

Percentage of population

Japan's narrow-based, bulging pyramid shows an older population with relatively few young people. The birth rate is low and the population is falling.

Uganda's sloping pyramid shows the country has a high birth rate, many children, few older people, and a fast-growing population.

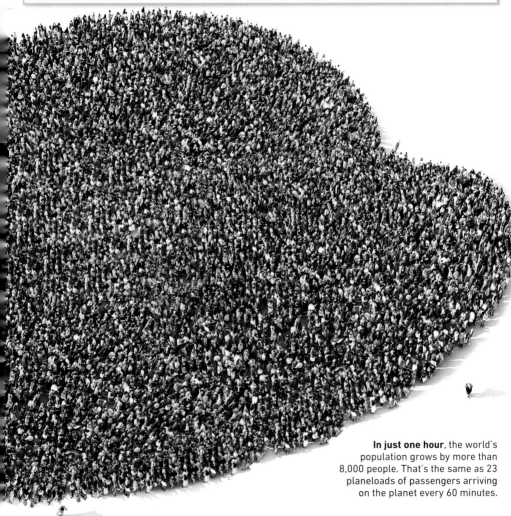

In just one hour, the world's population grows by more than 8,000 people. That's the same as 23 planeloads of passengers arriving on the planet every 60 minutes.

RUSSIA IS THE BIGGEST COUNTRY BUT RANKS ONLY **NINTH** IN TERMS OF POPULATION SIZE.

BY 2030, ABOUT **60%** OF THE WORLD'S POPULATION WILL BE LIVING IN CITIES.

Humans and other life forms

Earth is rich in wonderful life forms—including us! Our bodies perform fantastic feats each day just to keep us alive. We share our world with a host of other incredible plants and animals—some massive, others tiny—many of which have extraordinary abilities.

The manta ray is a gentle giant that "flies" through the water by beating its huge winglike fins. A manta can grow up to 30 ft (9 m) from fin tip to fin tip—much wider than a giraffe is tall!

HOW MUCH BLOOD DOES
A HEART PUMP?

The average **adult human heart** pumps about **10.6 pints** (5 liters) of blood **every minute**, which is the **total amount** of blood in a **man's body**.

The heart has a left and a right side. The right side delivers blood to the lungs to pick up oxygen. The left side pumps this oxygen-rich blood around the body to deliver nutrients to all the body's cells. The cells absorb the oxygen, and the oxygen-poor blood returns to the heart to start its journey again.

Oxygen-poor blood returns to the heart through veins (shown in blue).

EXTREME PHYSIQUES

When cyclist Miguel Induráin won five Tours de France in the 1990s, his heart could pump 106 pints (50 liters) of blood a minute and his lungs could hold 16.9 pints (8 liters) of oxygen. Average adult lungs hold less than 12.7 pints (6 liters).

The muscle that makes up the wall of the heart has its own blood supply.

THERE ARE **EIGHT** BLOOD GROUPS ALTOGETHER, WITH O THE WORLD'S MOST COMMON GROUP.

THE LUB-DUB SOUND OF THE **BEATING HEART** IS CAUSED BY THE HEART'S VALVES OPENING AND CLOSING.

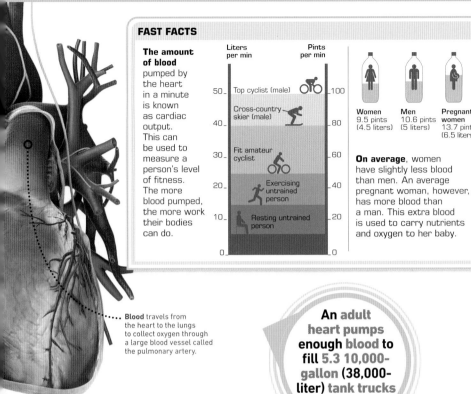

FAST FACTS

The amount of blood pumped by the heart in a minute is known as cardiac output. This can be used to measure a person's level of fitness. The more blood pumped, the more work their bodies can do.

Liters per min		Pints per min
50	Top cyclist (male)	100
40	Cross-country skier (male)	80
30	Fit amateur cyclist	60
20	Exercising untrained person	40
10	Resting untrained person	20
0		0

Women
9.5 pints
(4.5 liters)

Men
10.6 pints
(5 liters)

Pregnant women
13.7 pints
(6.5 liters)

On average, women have slightly less blood than men. An average pregnant woman, however, has more blood than a man. This extra blood is used to carry nutrients and oxygen to her baby.

Blood travels from the heart to the lungs to collect oxygen through a large blood vessel called the pulmonary artery.

An adult heart pumps enough blood to fill 5.3 10,000-gallon (38,000-liter) tank trucks every month.

The heart pumps oxygen-rich blood to the body through arteries (shown in red). This blood is bright red because it contains hemoglobin, the substance that carries the oxygen. Oxygen-poor blood is dark red.

THE BLUE WHALE, THE WORLD'S LARGEST ANIMAL, HAS A HEART THE SIZE OF A MOTORCYCLE.

OCTOPUSES AND HORSESHOE CRABS HAVE BLUE BLOOD BECAUSE THEY HAVE COPPER INSTEAD OF IRON IN THEIR BLOODSTREAMS.

HOW LONG ARE YOUR
BLOOD VESSELS?

It is estimated that there may be as many as **100,000 miles** (160,000 km) of blood vessels in an **adult's body** and **60,000 miles** (97,000 km) in a **child's**.

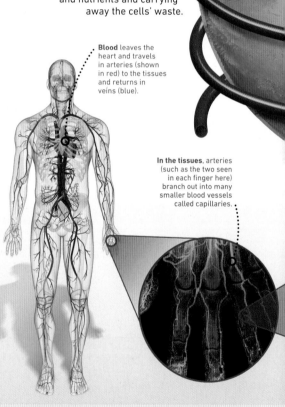

There are three main types of blood vessels: arteries, veins, and capillaries. They cover such a great distance because they need to reach almost every cell in your body, delivering oxygen and nutrients and carrying away the cells' waste.

Blood leaves the heart and travels in arteries (shown in red) to the tissues and returns in veins (blue).

In the tissues, arteries (such as the two seen in each finger here) branch out into many smaller blood vessels called capillaries.

COLD FINGERS

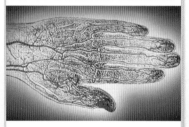

Although arteries (shown in red in this false-color scan) reach to the ends of the fingers, sometimes hands can feel cold. This is because the body may restrict the blood flow to the hands to keep the rest of the body warm.

RED BONE MARROW INSIDE BONES MAKES ABOUT **2.4 MILLION** NEW RED BLOOD CELLS A SECOND.

RED BLOOD CELLS MAKE UP **40%** OF BLOOD—AND ABOUT 5,000 OF THEM WOULD FILL THIS PERIOD.

An adult human's **network of blood vessels** would circle the world **four times.**

Capillaries are thin—about 20 of the narrowest can fit across the width of a hair. These are just wide enough for one red blood cell to travel through at a time. Their thin walls let substances pass between the blood and the body tissues.

FAST FACTS

Blood cell

Capillary

Some capillaries are so narrow that only one blood cell at a time can pass through them. The widest blood vessel is an artery called the aorta. At its widest, the aorta is about 1.2 in (3 cm) across—about 6,000 times wider than the narrowest capillary.

Veins 65% of blood volume

Arteries 35% of blood volume

There is more blood in the body's veins than in the arteries at any one time. Veins are wider inside than arteries (because they have thinner walls), and blood moves more slowly through them.

London to Cologne
309 miles (498 km)

A red blood cell is thought to travel 2.5 miles (4 km) around your body every day. Over its lifetime of about 120 days, a cell will cover 300 miles (480 km)—that's just under the distance from London to Cologne.

EVERY **CELL** IN THE HUMAN BODY RECEIVES BLOOD FROM THE HEART EXCEPT THE CORNEA AT THE FRONT OF THE EYES.

THE BLUE WHALE IS SO BIG THAT ITS **AORTA** ALONE IS ABOUT THE SAME SIZE AS A DINNER PLATE.

HOW HEAVY ARE
YOUR BONES?

Bones are actually very **light**—your **skeleton** accounts for only about **15 percent** of your **total weight**.

An **adult human** weighs more than **six times** the weight of its skeleton.

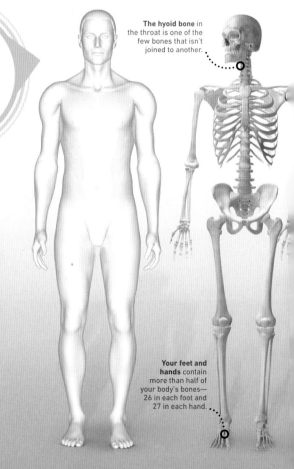

The **hyoid bone** in the throat is one of the few bones that isn't joined to another.

Your **feet and hands** contain more than half of your body's bones— 26 in each foot and 27 in each hand.

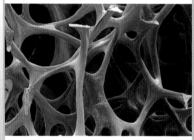

INSIDE A BONE

Although very strong, bones are light because they are not solid. Inside the hard, dense, compact bone is spongy bone, which looks like honeycomb (shown here in this false-colored image). The spaces in the bone are filled with jellylike marrow.

FLEXIBLE COLLAGEN INSIDE BONE KEEPS RENEWING ITSELF, RESULTING IN A NEW SKELETON ABOUT EVERY 10 YEARS!

THE SKULL CONSISTS OF 22 BONES, BUT THE MANDIBLE (LOWER JAW) IS THE ONLY ONE THAT CAN MOVE.

FAST FACTS

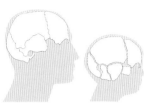

Adult skull   **Baby skull**

Babies are born with around 300 bones. As they grow up, many of the bones—such as those in the skull—fuse together, so most adults have 206 bones.

3,821 lb
(1,733 kg)

Piece of bone

Bone is incredibly strong. A cube of bone measuring 0.4 in (1 cm) along each side would be able to support 3,821 lb (1,733 kg)—the weight of an adult male hippo.

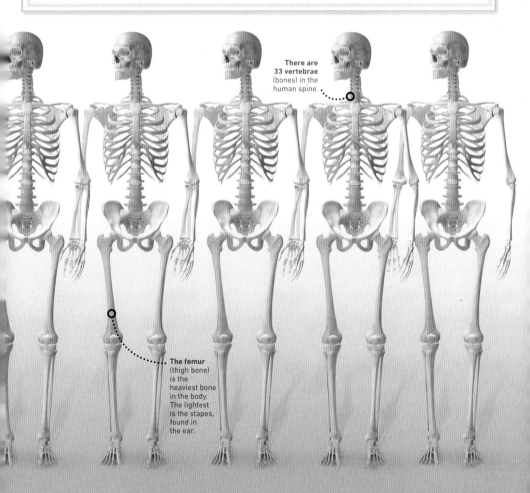

There are 33 vertebrae (bones) in the human spine.

The femur (thigh bone) is the heaviest bone in the body. The lightest is the stapes, found in the ear.

PEOPLE ARE 0.2 IN (0.5 CM) **TALLER** IN THE MORNING BECAUSE THE BACKBONE HASN'T HAD TO SUPPORT THE BODY'S WEIGHT DURING SLEEP.

A **GIRAFFE** HAS SEVEN NECK BONES, WHICH IS EXACTLY THE SAME NUMBER OF NECK BONES AS HUMANS!

FAST FACTS

Large eyes give animals the brightest, sharpest vision possible. Tarsiers own some of the largest eyes relative to their body size. They need them to hunt for insects in the rainforest at night. Each of their eyes is as big as their brain! A human's eyes are proportionally much smaller.

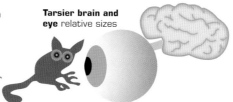

Tarsier brain and eye relative sizes

Human brain and eye relative sizes

WHAT HAS THE
BIGGEST EYES?

The **colossal squid**, a little-known species of squid bigger than the giant squid, has **eyes** up to **11 in** (27 cm) across in the few individuals measured.

PREHISTORIC VISION

Extinct reptiles called ichthyosaurs had eyes up to 12 in (30 cm) across. Like huge squid species, some probably hunted in the deep sea, their big eyes helping them see in the dim light.

Human eyeball (life size) 1 in (2.4 cm) across

Horse eyeball (life size) 2 in (4 cm) across

BOYS ARE MORE LIKELY TO BE COLOR-BLIND THAN GIRLS, WHICH MEANS THEY HAVE PROBLEMS SEEING SHADES OF RED AND GREEN.

A HUMAN EYE **BLINKS** AT LEAST 15 TIMES A MINUTE TO CLEAN AND PROTECT IT.

The lens of the colossal squid's eye is ball-shaped and about the size of an orange.

The largest **colossal squid eye** ever studied had the same diameter as **11 human eyeballs.**

Blue whale eyeball (life size) 6 in (15 cm) across

Colossal squid eyeball (life size) 11 in (27 cm) across. Experts think the colossal squid's eyes may grow to 12–16 in (30–40 cm) across—as big as a beach ball!

BROWN IS THE MOST COMMON EYE COLOR IN THE WORLD, FOUND IN MORE THAN HALF THE GLOBAL POPULATION.

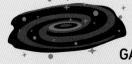

THE **NAKED EYE** CAN SEE THE ANDROMEDA GALAXY—A MIND-BOGGLING 2.5 MILLION LIGHT-YEARS AWAY.

WHAT HAS THE
BIGGEST TEETH?

African elephants have the **biggest teeth** of all animals. They have **enormous chewing teeth**—which they use to crush vegetation—and **huge front teeth** called **tusks**.

Up to 10 deep ridges line the top of the African elephant's molar, ideal for grinding tree branches.

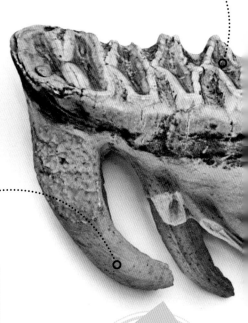

The roots sit below the surface of the gum. When the molar first forms, the roots point down, but as the tooth moves forward in the jaw, the roots slant backward.

VIPERFISH TEETH

A viperfish's teeth are so long, they curve around the outside of its head when it closes its mouth. The glassy daggers are ideal for catching fish that live in the darkest depths of the ocean.

Around **65 human molars** can fit on top of one elephant molar.

Human molars are on average 0.75 in (2 cm) from the crown to the root. Humans grow only two sets of teeth in their lifetime.

THE OCEAN-DWELLING **RAINBOW SLUG** GOES THROUGH AT LEAST 700,000 TEETH— A RECORD IN THE ANIMAL KINGDOM.

THE **GARDEN SNAIL** HAS MORE THAN 14,000 TEETH DURING ITS LIFETIME— MORE THAN ANY OTHER LAND ANIMAL.

An elephant has four molars (back teeth) in its jaws at any one time. They grow up to 8.3 in (21 cm) long and 2.75 in (7 cm) wide and weigh up to 9 lb (4 kg). The teeth wear down and are replaced six times during the elephant's life.

The crown is the part of a tooth that sits above the gum.

FAST FACTS

Tusks are front teeth used for defense while fighting, digging, lifting, or displaying. Walruses also use theirs like ice picks to haul themselves out of the water.

African elephant tusk
10 ft (3 m)

Narwhal tusk 9 ft (2.7 m)

Walrus tusk 3.3 ft (1 m)

Warthog tusk 18 in (45 cm)

Babirusa tusk 12 in (30 cm)

An ancient sharklike fish called *Helicoprion* had no teeth in its upper jaw and a unique set in its lower jaw, which were arranged like a spiral saw. No one is sure how the fish used them. Perhaps the teeth shredded the flesh of the fish's prey as it pushed it toward its throat to swallow it.

Saw teeth spiraled out of its mouth

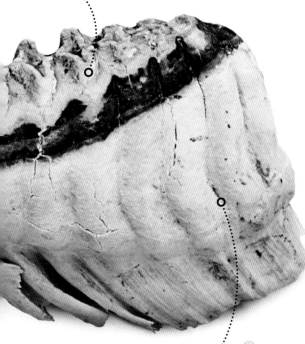

The creases in the root show that a molar is made up of a collection of up to 12 separate plates, or tooth buds, that merged together as they grew.

A lion's back teeth are around 1 in (3 cm) wide. They are razor-sharp and work in pairs, like scissors, to slice through meat.

A great white shark has serrated teeth. The largest can grow to 2.75 in (7 cm) from base to tip.

All teeth are shown life size

STRAWBERRIES ARE A NATURAL TEETH CLEANER BECAUSE THEIR ACIDS CAN GET RID OF STAINS.

WHALE SHARKS ARE THE WORLD'S BIGGEST FISH, BUT THEY HAVE TEENY-TINY TEETH MEASURING ONLY 0.2 IN (6 MM) LONG.

Body data

ORGANIZING THE BODY

Cells, the building blocks of the body, organize themselves into more **complex structures** called **tissues**. Tissues, in turn, combine to form **organs**, which make up the **systems** that **control the body's functions**. The body has **many different systems**, including the nervous system (right).

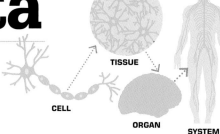

TISSUE

CELL

ORGAN

SYSTEM

VITAL INGREDIENTS

An average adult human contains:

enough **phosphorus** to make **220 matches**

enough **iron** to make a

nail 3 in (7 cm) long

enough **carbon** to fill **900 pencils**

enough **fat** for **75 candles**

KEEPING US COMPANY

In an average human body, there are approximately

100 trillion cells.

But each person is also home to around **10 times this number of bacteria**. Gathered together, these bacteria would fill a **0.5-gallon (2-liter) jug**.

BREATHE DEEPLY

The rate at which humans breathe depends on what they're doing—ranging from about **12–15 breaths per minute** while **resting** to **45–50 breaths per minute** when **exercising hard**.

AT LEAST **93%** OF YOUR BODY CONSISTS OF THREE KEY CHEMICAL ELEMENTS: OXYGEN (65%), CARBON (18.5%), AND HYDROGEN (10%).

10%
18.5%
65%
6.5%

THE HUMAN BODY IS HOME TO A TINY AMOUNT OF GOLD, FOUND MOSTLY IN THE BLOODSTREAM.

IN THEIR LIFETIME, **THE AVERAGE HUMAN WILL:**

• grow 92 ft (**28 m**) of fingernails—just a little longer than a standard-sized swimming pool
• spend a total of **3 years** on the toilet • produce **10,500 gallons** (40,000 liters) of urine • work for **9 years** • shed around **550 lb** (250 kg) of dead skin • blink **415 million** times • talk for **12 years** • grow **590 miles** (950 km) of hair on their head—that's around the length of the UK!

REPRODUCTION

• Elephants have a long gestation period—they carry a single baby for **22 months** before giving birth.

• Termite queens can lay up to **30,000 eggs** a day.

• The ocean sunfish can produce more eggs than any other known vertebrate. Each breeding season, the fish scatters up to **300 million tiny eggs** into the ocean.

FEEDING TIME

An adult blue whale can eat as much as **3.8 tons (3.5 tonnes)** of krill (tiny crustaceans) in a single day—about the weight of **3 small cars.**

Adult mayflies eat nothing at all. They live no longer than a day!

BIG & SMALL

An adult human body contains

206 bones.

The **longest** is the femur in the upper leg. The shortest are three tiny bones called ossicles in the ear.

EAR OSSICLES (ACTUAL SIZE)

FEMUR (ACTUAL SIZE)

HEARING RANGES

HUMANS
20 Hz–20,000 Hz

DOGS
40 Hz–45,000 Hz

BATS
2,000 Hz–110,000 Hz

| 0 Hz | 10 Hz | 100 Hz | 1,000 Hz | 10,000 Hz | 100,000 Hz |

SOME WHITE BLOOD CELLS THAT FIGHT INFECTION LAST LESS THAN ONE DAY, WHILE SOME NERVE CELLS IN THE BRAIN LAST A LIFETIME.

THE DIGESTIVE SYSTEM MEASURES AT LEAST 23 FT (7 M) FROM THE MOUTH TO THE BOTTOM.

WHAT IS THE
BIGGEST ANIMAL?

The **largest animal** on the **planet** is the **blue whale** measuring **100 ft** (30 m). It is the **heaviest** animal that has **ever lived**, including **dinosaurs**.

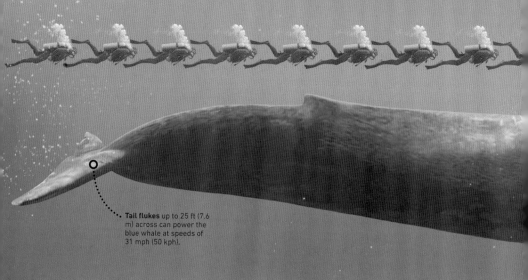

Tail flukes up to 25 ft (7.6 m) across can power the blue whale at speeds of 31 mph (50 kph).

FAST FACTS

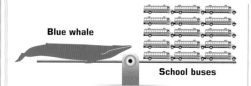

Blue whale

School buses

A blue whale is longer than a basketball court and weighs up to 200 tons (180 tonnes)—the same as 15 school buses.

Blue whales make a noise louder than a jet aircraft taking off. Whales produce very low frequency sounds at a level of 188 decibels that can be heard from thousands of miles away.

188 dB

140 dB

BLUE WHALES ARE NAMED AFTER THEIR PALE, BLOTCHY SKIN THAT LOOKS BRILLIANTLY BLUE UNDERWATER.

A WHISTLING SOUND IS MADE BY BLUE WHALES TO EXPRESS EMOTIONS OR ATTRACT OTHER BLUE WHALES.

FILTER FEEDING

A blue whale can eat around 4 tons (3.5 tonnes) of tiny sea creatures, called krill, a day. Taking 99-ton (90-tonne) gulps of water, the whale then filters the water out through baleen plates—comblike structures that hang from its jaw, trapping the krill.

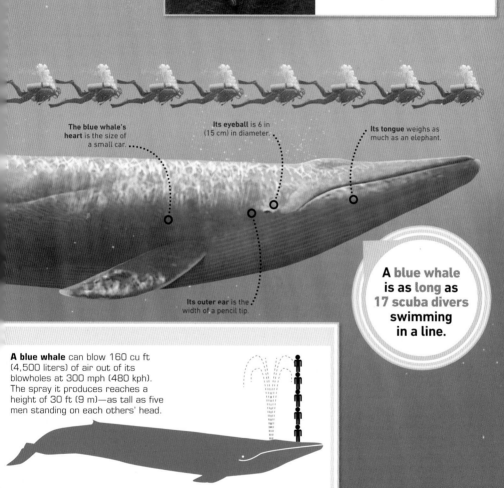

The blue whale's heart is the size of a small car.

Its eyeball is 6 in (15 cm) in diameter.

Its tongue weighs as much as an elephant.

Its outer ear is the width of a pencil tip.

A blue whale is as long as 17 scuba divers swimming in a line.

A blue whale can blow 160 cu ft (4,500 liters) of air out of its blowholes at 300 mph (480 kph). The spray it produces reaches a height of 30 ft (9 m)—as tall as five men standing on each others' head.

A BLUE WHALE'S TRAVELING **SPEED** IS ABOUT 5 MPH (8 KPH), BUT IT CAN SWIM AT 20 MPH (32 KPH) FOR SHORT PERIODS.

BLUE WHALES LIVE FOR ABOUT **90 YEARS**—SCIENTISTS CAN WORK OUT THE AGE BY COUNTING THE AMOUNT OF EARWAX!

WHAT WAS THE
BIGGEST DINOSAUR?

The **fossil bones** of *Patagotitan*, one of the **largest animals ever to walk on land**, were discovered in 2014. It is a type of **titanosaur** that **fossil hunters** estimate weighed up to **77 tons** (70 tonnes) and measured **122 ft** (37 m) long.

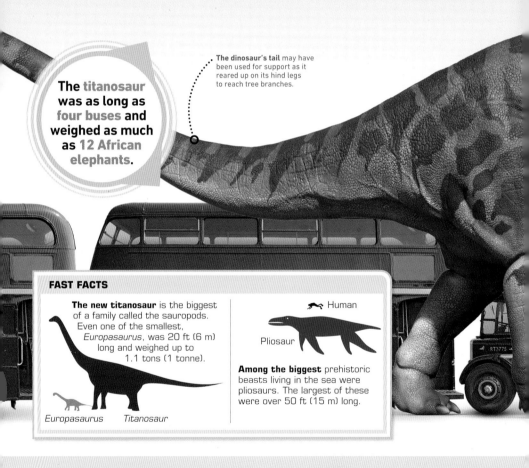

The **titanosaur** was as long as **four buses** and weighed as much as **12 African elephants**.

The dinosaur's tail may have been used for support as it reared up on its hind legs to reach tree branches.

FAST FACTS

The new titanosaur is the biggest of a family called the sauropods. Even one of the smallest, *Europasaurus*, was 20 ft (6 m) long and weighed up to 1.1 tons (1 tonne).

Europasaurus   *Titanosaur*

Human

Pliosaur

Among the biggest prehistoric beasts living in the sea were pliosaurs. The largest of these were over 50 ft (15 m) long.

IN 1842, SCIENTIST RICHARD OWEN NAMED THESE PREHISTORIC CREATURES DINOSAURS, GREEK FOR "TERRIBLE LIZARDS."

TITANOSAURS WERE COLOSSAL, BUT THEIR **EGGS** WERE NO BIGGER THAN OSTRICH EGGS!

BEFORE THE DINOSAURS

Long before the dinosaurs, there were no large animals on land—but there were in the oceans. *Pterygotus*, a giant sea scorpion that lived 400 million years ago, grew to 7.5 ft (2.3 m) long—bigger than an adult human.

The fossil bones were discovered in Patagonia, southern Argentina. The bones revealed that the titanosaur was a teenager and was still growing!

The small head did not contain heavy jaws for chewing food—titanosaurs simply gulped it down.

Its long neck meant that the titanosaur could eat from the ground or from trees. It had to eat a lot—a dumpster full of vegetation every day.

Patagotitan
122 ft (37 m) long

Double-decker bus
31.2 ft (9.5 m) long

SCIENTISTS ESTIMATE THE SIZE OF *PATAGOTITAN* BY STUDYING ITS BONES— THE **THIGH BONE** ALONE WAS ABOUT 8 FT (2.4 M) LONG.

NOT ALL TITANOSAURS WERE GIANTS; SOME, INCLUDING *SALTASAURUS*, WERE **NO BIGGER** THAN A BUS!

WHAT WAS THE
BIGGEST LAND PREDATOR?

One of the **biggest predators** that ever lived **on land** was *Spinosaurus*, a 59-ft- (18-m-) long dinosaur.

Spinosaurus lived around 100 million years ago. It preyed on fish as well as other animals, including dinosaurs.

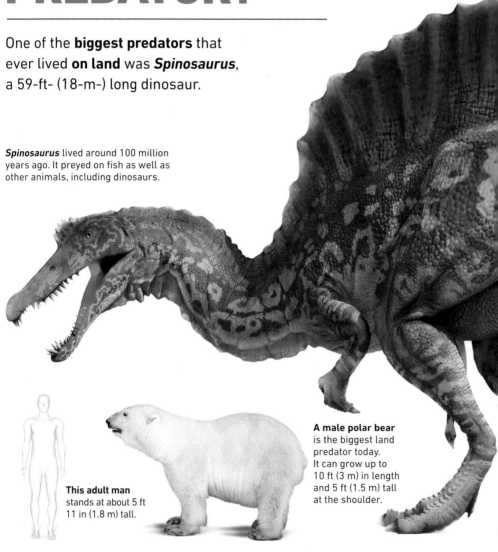

This adult man stands at about 5 ft 11 in (1.8 m) tall.

A male polar bear is the biggest land predator today. It can grow up to 10 ft (3 m) in length and 5 ft (1.5 m) tall at the shoulder.

TINY HOLES AT THE END OF *SPINOSAURUS'S* SNOUT MAY HAVE HELPED IT DETECT FISH IN THE MURKY WATERS.

SPINOSAURUS HAD LARGE, POINTED TEETH THAT WERE PERFECT FOR CATCHING SLIPPERY FISH.

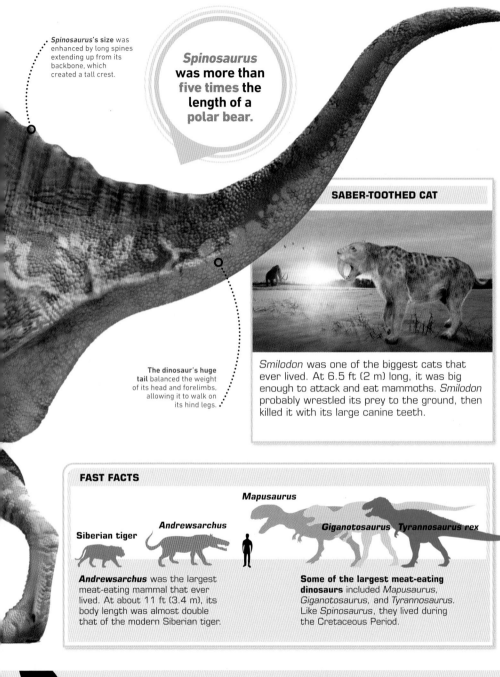

Spinosaurus's size was enhanced by long spines extending up from its backbone, which created a tall crest.

Spinosaurus **was more than five times the length of a polar bear.**

The dinosaur's huge **tail** balanced the weight of its head and forelimbs, allowing it to walk on its hind legs.

SABER-TOOTHED CAT

Smilodon was one of the biggest cats that ever lived. At 6.5 ft (2 m) long, it was big enough to attack and eat mammoths. *Smilodon* probably wrestled its prey to the ground, then killed it with its large canine teeth.

FAST FACTS

Siberian tiger   *Andrewsarchus*   *Mapusaurus*   *Giganotosaurus*   *Tyrannosaurus rex*

Andrewsarchus was the largest meat-eating mammal that ever lived. At about 11 ft (3.4 m), its body length was almost double that of the modern Siberian tiger.

Some of the largest meat-eating dinosaurs included *Mapusaurus*, *Giganotosaurus*, and *Tyrannosaurus*. Like *Spinosaurus*, they lived during the Cretaceous Period.

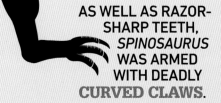

AS WELL AS RAZOR-SHARP TEETH, *SPINOSAURUS* WAS ARMED WITH DEADLY CURVED CLAWS.

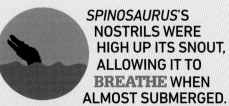

SPINOSAURUS'S NOSTRILS WERE HIGH UP ITS SNOUT, ALLOWING IT TO BREATHE WHEN ALMOST SUBMERGED.

WHAT WAS THE
BIGGEST SNAKE?

Titanoboa was an **enormous snake** measuring **48 ft** (14.6 m), or longer than a school bus. It lived around **60 million years ago** in the **jungle swamps** of modern-day **Colombia**.

Titanoboa's **coloring** is unknown. The pattern on this illustration is based on the anaconda, one of the biggest snakes alive today.

Snakes breathe through a hole called the glottis. This can move to the side so that the reptile can breathe as it slowly swallows its prey.

EATING HABITS

Big snakes such as pythons can eat prey wider than themselves. The snake cannot chew, so prey must be swallowed whole. Digesting food uses so much energy, the snake is inactive for several days.

LIKE THE JAWS OF TODAY'S SNAKES, THE **LOWER JAW** WAS FLEXIBLE, ENABLING *TITANOBOA* TO SWALLOW PREY WHOLE.

TITANOBOA **FEASTED** ON CROCODILES, GIANT TURTLES, AND FISH.

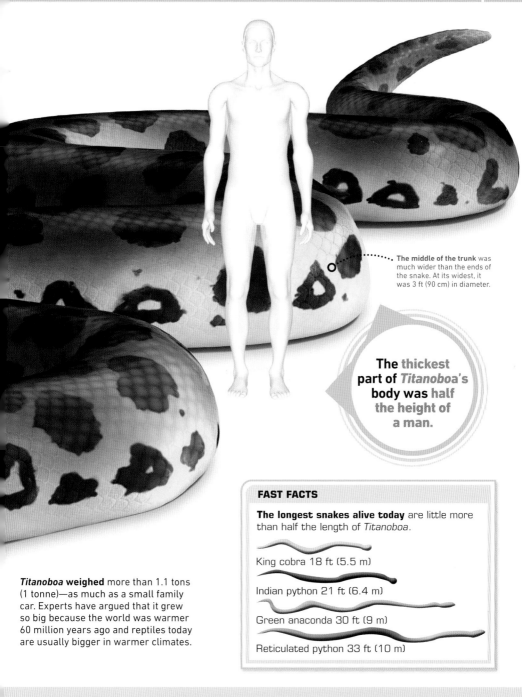

The middle of the trunk was much wider than the ends of the snake. At its widest, it was 3 ft (90 cm) in diameter.

The **thickest** part of *Titanoboa's* **body was half the height of a man.**

FAST FACTS

The longest snakes alive today are little more than half the length of *Titanoboa*.

King cobra 18 ft (5.5 m)

Indian python 21 ft (6.4 m)

Green anaconda 30 ft (9 m)

Reticulated python 33 ft (10 m)

Titanoboa **weighed** more than 1.1 tons (1 tonne)—as much as a small family car. Experts have argued that it grew so big because the world was warmer 60 million years ago and reptiles today are usually bigger in warmer climates.

THE JAWS WERE PACKED WITH CURVED TEETH— PERFECT FOR HOLDING ONTO PREY!

WHEN THE FOSSILS WERE FIRST DISCOVERED, THEY WERE MISTAKENLY IDENTIFIED AS THOSE OF CROCODILES.

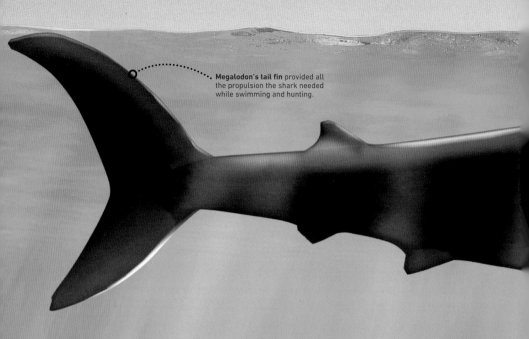

Megalodon's tail fin provided all the propulsion the shark needed while swimming and hunting.

MOSASAUR

Megalodon was one of the world's biggest-ever hunters, but many other ocean predators have grown to monstrous lengths. The 49-ft (15-m) *Mosasaurus* lived around 65 million years ago.

HOW BIG WAS THE
BIGGEST SHARK?

The **largest shark** that ever lived was **megalodon**, which may have grown to **66 ft (20 m) long**. It died out more than **1.5 million years ago**.

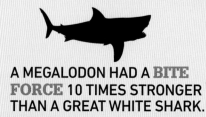

A MEGALODON HAD A **BITE FORCE** 10 TIMES STRONGER THAN A GREAT WHITE SHARK.

THREE MEGALODONS HAD A **MASS** SIMILAR TO A COMMERCIAL AIRPLANE.

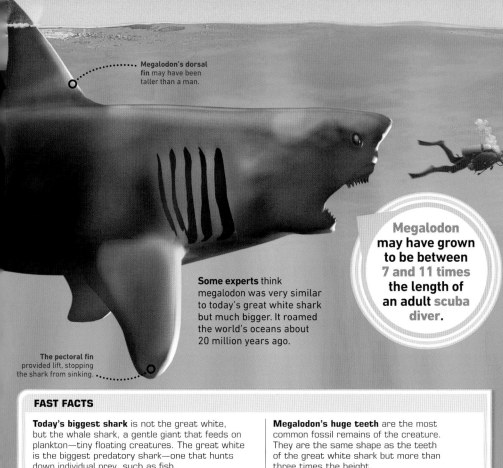

Megalodon's dorsal fin may have been taller than a man.

Some experts think megalodon was very similar to today's great white shark but much bigger. It roamed the world's oceans about 20 million years ago.

The pectoral fin provided lift, stopping the shark from sinking.

Megalodon may have grown to be between **7 and 11 times the length of an adult scuba diver.**

FAST FACTS

Today's biggest shark is not the great white, but the whale shark, a gentle giant that feeds on plankton—tiny floating creatures. The great white is the biggest predatory shark—one that hunts down individual prey, such as fish.

Megalodon's huge teeth are the most common fossil remains of the creature. They are the same shape as the teeth of the great white shark but more than three times the height.

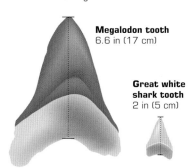

Megalodon
52–66 ft
(16–20 m) long,
55 tons (50 tonnes)

Whale shark
59 ft (18 m) long,
22 tons (20 tonnes)

Great white shark
23 ft (7 m) long,
2 tons (2 tonnes)

Megalodon tooth
6.6 in (17 cm)

Great white shark tooth
2 in (5 cm)

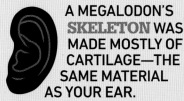

A MEGALODON'S **SKELETON** WAS MADE MOSTLY OF CARTILAGE—THE SAME MATERIAL AS YOUR EAR.

SHARKS HAVE BEEN AROUND FOR AT LEAST 450 MILLION YEARS— LONG BEFORE DINOSAURS EVOLVED.

Pedipalps are not legs—they are long mouthparts.

The spider's legspan is measured from the tip of the first leg on one side to the tip of the fourth leg on the other.

The spider's fangs are tucked under the hair-covered upper mouthparts.

The hairs covering the spider's body can cause rashes and swelling on human skin. This part, the abdomen, has hairs that the spider can flick at attackers to defend itself.

The Goliath birdeater is a species of tarantula that lives in South America. It grows big enough to eat birds, although it mostly eats insects, rodents, bats, snakes, and lizards. The spider pounces on prey and injects it with venom from its fangs.

A FEMALE GOLIATH SPIDER HAS A **LIFESPAN** OF UP TO 20 YEARS.

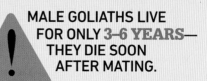

MALE GOLIATHS LIVE FOR ONLY **3–6 YEARS**— THEY DIE SOON AFTER MATING.

Goliaths **can grow to be bigger than an adult's hand and can cover a dinner plate!**

GIANT HUNTSMAN SPIDER

The longest spider legs are thought to belong to the giant huntsman spider of Laos, Southeast Asia. Its legs span up to 12 in (30 cm), although its body is just 1.8 in (4.6 cm) long.

HOW BIG CAN SPIDERS GROW?

The **heaviest type** of spider is the **Goliath birdeater**, which can **weigh** up to **6 oz** (175 g). The biggest measured had a **legspan** of **11 in** (28 cm).

The Goliath birdeater rubs bristles on its legs to produce a hissing sound as a warning to predators.

FAST FACTS

Darwin's bark spiders can spin webs as wide as a six-lane highway (80 ft/25 m). Its silk is highly resistant to breaking and more than 10 times tougher than Kevlar (a material used to make body armor).

All spiders are venomous, and some species have venom that is deadly enough to kill dozens of mice. Most spiders are harmless to humans, but these three demand respect!

Mice killed by 1 thousandth of a gram

Southern black widow 12.5 mice

Mediterranean black widow 37 mice

Brazilian wandering spider 41 mice

GOLIATHS CAN'T DIGEST SOLID FOOD— THEY LIQUEFY THE INSIDES OF THEIR PREY AND THEN SUCK IT DRY.

THE GOLIATH'S FANGS ARE 0.8 IN (2 CM) LONG. FOR HUMANS, A BITE FROM THE FANGS IS LIKE A WASP STING.

WHAT IS THE
BIGGEST
INSECT?

There are several contenders, but the **Atlas moth** has the biggest wings, with a **span** of **10 in** (25 cm) and a **wing area** of **62 sq in** (400 sq cm).

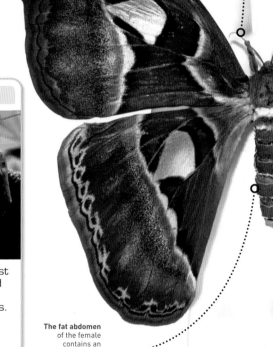

These narrow antennae tell us this is a female, which is even larger and heavier than a male. The male has bigger, more feathery antennae and uses them to detect pheromones (scent) released by females.

The fat abdomen of the female contains an egg factory.

GIANT WETA

The giant weta, one of the world's heaviest insects, lives in New Zealand. Wetas feed mostly on fresh leaves in their forest habitat and have grown to mouselike sizes. At 2.5 oz (70 g), the largest are as big as three house mice.

THE MOTH IS NAMED AFTER THE GREEK GOD **ATLAS**, WHO CARRIED THE WORLD ON HIS SHOULDERS.

THE CATERPILLARS ARE MASSIVE, TOO— THEY MUNCH ON **LEAVES** EVERY MINUTE OF THE DAY.

The Atlas moth of Southeast Asia is the biggest insect by wing area. However, the white witch moth of Central and South America has the widest wingspan, at about 12 in (31 cm).

> The Atlas moth is much bigger than an adult human hand.

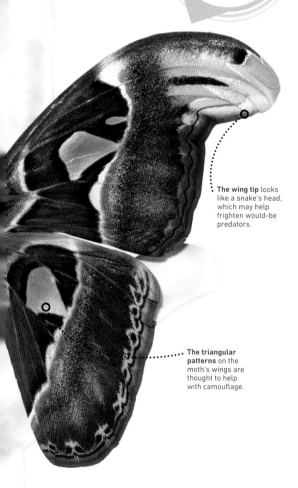

The **wing tip** looks like a snake's head, which may help frighten would-be predators.

The **triangular patterns** on the moth's wings are thought to help with camouflage.

FAST FACTS

There are other insects competing for the title of the biggest insect alive. Here are some of the contenders.

The titan beetle of South America's rainforests grows up to 6.5 in (16.5 cm) long—as long as the body of a rat. Its jaws can snap a pencil in half.

Rat

Titan beetle

Stick insects can be even longer. The record-breaking Chan's megastick of Borneo, Malaysia, is 22.3 in (56.7 cm) long with outstretched legs. That's longer than this book.

Goliath beetle grub

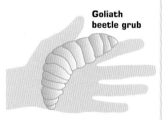

Some insects have really large grubs. One of the biggest and heaviest is that of Africa's Goliath beetle. It can grow up to 5 in (13 cm) long and weighs 3.5 oz (100 g).

AS AN ADULT, THE MOTH DOESN'T EAT—IT LIVES ON THE RESERVES STORED FROM WHEN IT WAS A **CATERPILLAR**.

ONCE IT RUNS **OUT OF ENERGY** TO POWER ITS HUGE WINGS, THE ATLAS MOTH DIES.

Running along the front edge of *Quetzalcoatlus*'s wing were the incredibly long bones of a single finger, which held the wing open.

The wings of *Quetzalcoatlus* stretched farther than those of a Tiger Moth biplane.

WHAT HAD THE
LONGEST
WINGS EVER?

The **largest flying creature** was a **pterosaur** called *Quetzalcoatlus*. It soared over its relatives, the **dinosaurs**, 68 million years ago. The largest had a **wingspan** of **more than 33 ft** (10 m).

FOR EACH **LONG TRIP**, *QUETZALCOATLUS* MAY HAVE BURNED OFF ABOUT 160 LB (72 KG) OF FAT.

THE PTEROSAUR MAY HAVE BEEN ABLE TO FLY **DISTANCES** OF UP TO 10,000 MILES (16,000 KM).

FAST FACTS

Here's how *Quetzalcoatlus*'s wingspan compares to some other giant flyers.

Quetzalcoatlus lived 68–66 million years ago and measured 33 ft (10 m) from wingtip to wingtip.

Argentavis lived 6 million years ago. With a wingspan of about 23 ft (7 m), it was one of the largest flying birds.

The great bustard is today's heaviest flying bird and has a wingspan of 8.2 ft (2.5 m).

The wandering albatross has the longest wings of any living bird, at 11.5 ft (3.5 m).

Quetzalcoatlus was very thin and light in the central body and neck, so despite its colossal dimensions, even this 33-ft (10-m) individual probably weighed less than 550 lb (250 kg). This is still twice as heavy as an ostrich.

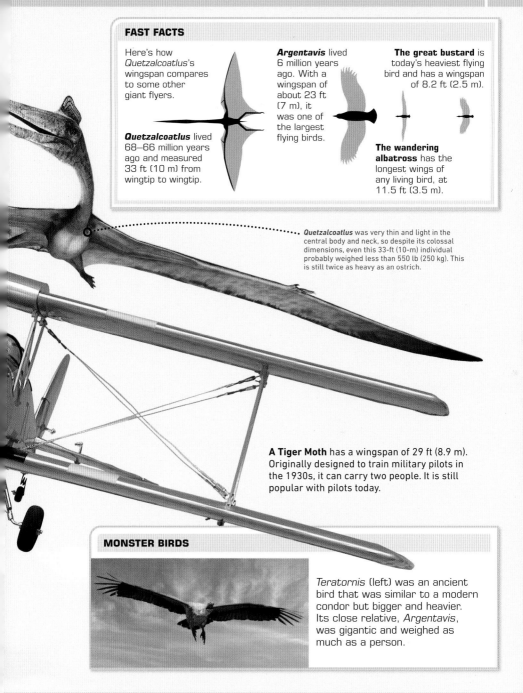

A Tiger Moth has a wingspan of 29 ft (8.9 m). Originally designed to train military pilots in the 1930s, it can carry two people. It is still popular with pilots today.

MONSTER BIRDS

Teratornis (left) was an ancient bird that was similar to a modern condor but bigger and heavier. Its close relative, *Argentavis*, was gigantic and weighed as much as a person.

QUETZALCOATLUS'S **BEAK** WAS ABOUT 8 FT (2.5 M) LONG— LONGER THAN AN ADULT PERSON!

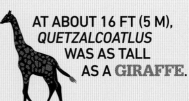

AT ABOUT 16 FT (5 M), *QUETZALCOATLUS* WAS AS TALL AS A **GIRAFFE**.

WHAT IS THE
SMALLEST BIRD?

The **bee hummingbird**, which lives only in Cuba, is **2.2 in** (5.5 cm) **long** and **weighs** just **0.06 oz** (1.6 g).

FAST FACTS

The bee hummingbird builds a cup-shaped nest about 1 in (2.5 cm) across from bits of cobwebs, bark, and lichen. Nests have been built on single clothes pegs.

Actual size

In contrast, the heaviest living bird that can fly is the great bustard. At 46 lb (20.9 kg), it weighs as much as a 6-year-old boy.

Great bustard

Elephant bird · Ostrich · Human · Chicken

Today's heaviest bird, the ostrich, can weigh nearly twice as much as an adult person. However, a few hundred years ago, an even heavier bird—the elephant bird—lived in Madagascar. It weighed as much as three ostriches. It is now extinct.

The **bee hummingbird is small** enough to perch on the end of a **pencil**.

The bee hummingbird is a tiny but busy bird. It hovers by flapping its wings at 80 times a second, with its heart beating at an incredible 1,220 times a minute. To power this activity, the bird must feed every 10–15 minutes. It eats about half its own body weight in sugary nectar every day.

THERE ARE MORE THAN 350 KNOWN SPECIES OF HUMMINGBIRD— ALL FOUND IN THE AMERICAS.

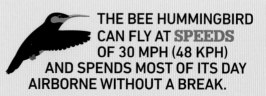

THE BEE HUMMINGBIRD CAN FLY AT SPEEDS OF 30 MPH (48 KPH) AND SPENDS MOST OF ITS DAY AIRBORNE WITHOUT A BREAK.

The male bee hummingbird has a glossy pink head and throat and is even smaller than the female.

SWORD-BILLED HUMMINGBIRD

Not all hummingbirds are tiny. Among the largest are sword-billed hummingbirds. Their bill alone measures the same as two entire bee hummingbirds!

HUMMINGBIRDS ARE THE ONLY BIRDS THAT CAN FLY BACKWARD—SOME CAN FLY UPSIDE DOWN, TOO!

THE METABOLISM OF A HUMMINGBIRD IS EQUAL TO AN AVERAGE MAN EATING 285 LB (129 KG) OF MEAT EVERY DAY!

WHICH BIRD LAID THE
BIGGEST EGG?

Eggs of the extinct **elephant bird** were up to **16 in** (40 cm) **long**. Elephant birds lived on the **island of Madagascar** alongside other supersized animals, including giant lemurs and giant tortoises.

Emu eggs are unusually dark. They look like a huge avocado, at 5 in (13 cm) high.

Emu

Kiwi

Rusty tinamou

Hummingbird

Chicken

King penguin

Quail

Cormorant

Common sandpiper

Tawny owl

The most familiar eggs are laid by the domestic chicken.

FAST FACTS

Elephant bird eggs are bigger than those of most dinosaurs. Even the eggs of sauropods (the biggest dinosaurs) are no more than 8 in (20 cm) long. Recent digs in China, however, appear to have turned up giant eggs of two-legged dinosaurs similar to *Oviraptor*.

24 in (60 cm)

16 in (40 cm)

8 in (20 cm)

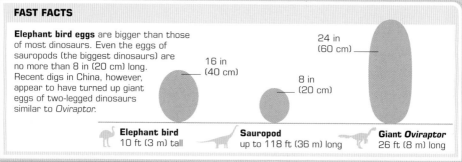

Elephant bird
10 ft (3 m) tall

Sauropod
up to 118 ft (36 m) long

Giant *Oviraptor*
26 ft (8 m) long

ABOUT 40 INTACT ELEPHANT BIRD EGGS HAVE BEEN FOUND.

ARGENTINOSAURUS WEIGHED 83 TONS (75 TONNES), BUT ITS EGGS WERE NO BIGGER THAN A SMALL MELON.

Elephant birds had died out about 1,000 years ago, though many of their eggshells still exist. Pieces found near the sites of ancient cooking fires suggest that people ate the eggs.

In terms of volume, an **elephant bird egg** is as big as **200 chicken eggs or 11 ostrich eggs.**

The shell of the egg is 0.15 in (3.8 mm) thick and could bear the weight of about 90 bricks (550 lb/248 kg).

Ostrich

The ostrich is the world's largest bird, and it lays the biggest eggs today—although they are the smallest in relation to the size of the mother. They weigh on average 3.1 lb (1.4 kg)—more than 20 chicken eggs.

Elephant bird

Cetti's warbler

KIWI EGGS

This X-ray of a female kiwi shows how much space her egg takes up inside her—kiwis lay the biggest eggs in relation to their body size.

Guillemot

Great auk

Carrion crow

Curlew

Sparrowhawk

Cuckoo

Redshank

A **KIWI** IS 20 TIMES SMALLER THAN AN EMU, BUT ITS EGGS ARE ALMOST THE SAME SIZE.

THE SMALLEST BIRD EGGS BELONG TO **HUMMINGBIRDS**— THEY ARE NO BIGGER THAN PEAS!

HOW FAR CAN A
BIRD FLY?

Bar-tailed godwits have been tracked flying **7,258 miles** (11,680 km) **nonstop** from Alaska to New Zealand on their **yearly migration**.

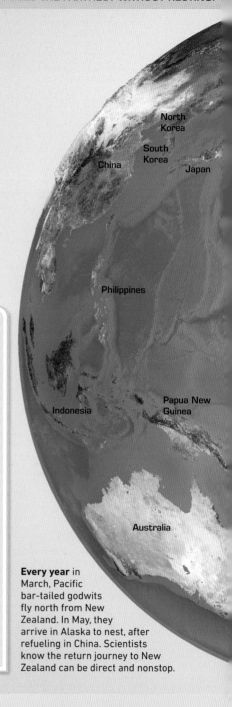

North Korea

South Korea

China

Japan

Philippines

Indonesia

Papua New Guinea

Australia

FAST FACTS

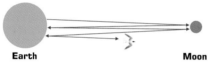

Earth   **Moon**

Arctic terns migrate from the Arctic to the Antarctic and back every year. Single birds have been tracked flying 44,100 miles (70,900 km) in this time. In their 30-year lifetime, they can cover 1.3 million miles (2.1 million km), or more than two round-trips to the Moon.

Glider 1,898 miles (3,055 km)

Airliner (Boeing 777 specially adapted for record attempt) 13,423 miles (21,602 km)

Breitling Orbiter balloon 25,361 miles (40,814 km)

Virgin Atlantic GlobalFlyer 25,766 miles (41,467 km)

An airliner can fly farther than any bird if it is specially adapted. Above are four human nonstop flight records involving different kinds of aircraft.

Every year in March, Pacific bar-tailed godwits fly north from New Zealand. In May, they arrive in Alaska to nest, after refueling in China. Scientists know the return journey to New Zealand can be direct and nonstop.

BAR-TAILED GODWITS SPEND TWO MONTHS AT THEIR BREEDING GROUND IN ALASKA, RAISING YOUNG AND REFUELING.

GODWITS FLAP THEIR LONG, SLEEK WINGS THROUGHOUT THEIR EPIC JOURNEY.

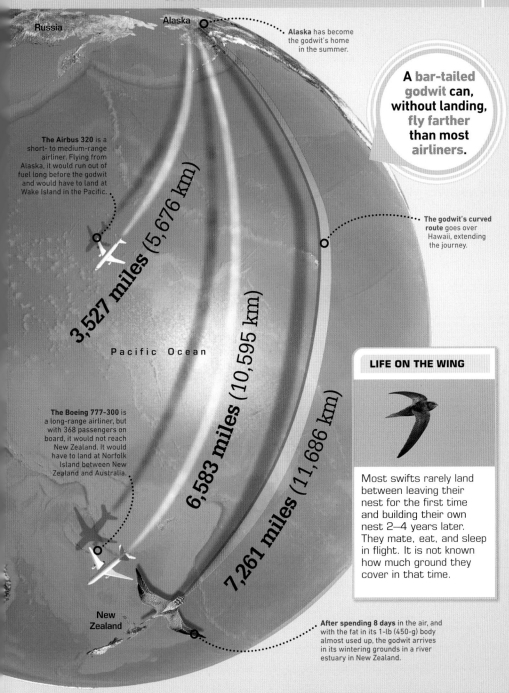

Russia

Alaska

Alaska has become the godwit's home in the summer.

A **bar-tailed godwit** can, **without landing, fly farther than most airliners.**

The Airbus 320 is a short- to medium-range airliner. Flying from Alaska, it would run out of fuel long before the godwit and would have to land at Wake Island in the Pacific.

The godwit's curved route goes over Hawaii, extending the journey.

3,527 miles (5,676 km)

Pacific Ocean

6,583 miles (10,595 km)

7,261 miles (11,686 km)

The Boeing 777-300 is a long-range airliner, but with 368 passengers on board, it would not reach New Zealand. It would have to land at Norfolk Island between New Zealand and Australia.

LIFE ON THE WING

Most swifts rarely land between leaving their nest for the first time and building their own nest 2—4 years later. They mate, eat, and sleep in flight. It is not known how much ground they cover in that time.

New Zealand

After spending 8 days in the air, and with the fat in its 1-lb (450-g) body almost used up, the godwit arrives in its wintering grounds in a river estuary in New Zealand.

THE GLOBE-TROTTING GODWITS FLY MORE THAN A QUARTER OF THE WAY AROUND THE WORLD IN **11 DAYS.**

IN 2022, A GODWIT FLEW FROM ALASKA TO TASMANIA—A **RECORD-BREAKING** DISTANCE OF 8,425 MILES (13,560 KM).

HOW OLD IS THE
OLDEST TREE?

The world's **oldest living tree** started life in around 3050 BCE, making it more than **5,065 years old.** The tree is a **Great Basin bristlecone pine** in the White Mountains of California.

1804 First steam locomotive is built

c.800 CE Vikings raid northwest Europe

The **oldest** bristlecone pine has lived through almost all of recorded **human** history.

OLDEST SEED

While excavating King Herod's Palace at Masada, Israel, in the 1960s, archaeologists found Judean date palm seeds that were at least 2,000 years old. In 2005, one seed successfully sprouted and was planted at Kibbutz Ketura. The tree has been nicknamed "Methuselah" after the Biblical man said to be the oldest person ever to live.

432 BCE Parthenon is completed in Greece

When the world's oldest tree sprouted from its seed, people wrote with pictures and symbols, not letters and words; the wheel was unknown in most of the world; and the great civilization of ancient Egypt was only just beginning.

c.3050 BCE The tree's seed sprouts

THE STINKY CORPSE FLOWER TAKES YEARS TO FLOWER BUT BLOOMS FOR ONLY A DAY OR TWO.

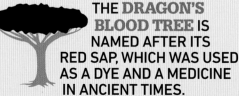

THE DRAGON'S BLOOD TREE IS NAMED AFTER ITS RED SAP, WHICH WAS USED AS A DYE AND A MEDICINE IN ANCIENT TIMES.

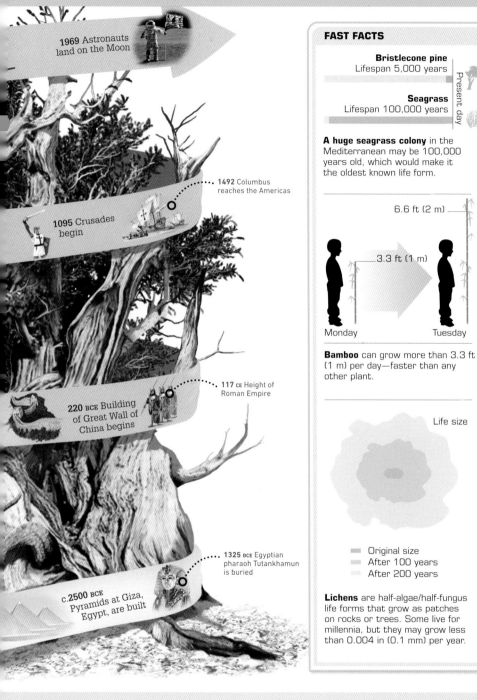

1969 Astronauts land on the Moon

1492 Columbus reaches the Americas

1095 Crusades begin

220 BCE Building of Great Wall of China begins

117 CE Height of Roman Empire

1325 BCE Egyptian pharaoh Tutankhamun is buried

c.2500 BCE Pyramids at Giza, Egypt, are built

FAST FACTS

Bristlecone pine
Lifespan 5,000 years

Seagrass
Lifespan 100,000 years

Present day

A huge seagrass colony in the Mediterranean may be 100,000 years old, which would make it the oldest known life form.

6.6 ft (2 m)

3.3 ft (1 m)

Monday   Tuesday

Bamboo can grow more than 3.3 ft (1 m) per day—faster than any other plant.

Life size

Original size
After 100 years
After 200 years

Lichens are half-algae/half-fungus life forms that grow as patches on rocks or trees. Some live for millennia, but they may grow less than 0.004 in (0.1 mm) per year.

THE **CANNONBALL TREE** BEARS WEIGHTY FRUITS THAT DROP OFF AND SMASH OPEN WITH A LOUD BANG.

GOATS INHABITING THE MOROCCAN VILLAGE OF TAMRI CLIMB 30 FT (9 M) INTO THE **ARGAN TREES** TO MUNCH ON BERRIES.

HOW OLD ARE THE
OLDEST ANIMALS?

Ocean quahog (clams) are known to live for more than **500 years**. Scientists think some **sponges** may live **even longer**.

ANCIENT SPONGES

It is difficult to identify the age of a sponge, but Caribbean giant barrel sponges (left) have very long lives; one is believed to be 2,300 years old. Some Antarctic glass sponges may live for more than 10,000 years.

Ocean quahogs can live nearly 6 times longer than Asian elephants.

Human
122 years

Rougheye rockfish
140–200 years

Most humans don't live 122 years, but there is a verified case of a woman who did.

Asian elephant
86 years

Olm
(a cave salamander)
100 years

Tuatara
119 years

THE ADULT MAYFLY HAS THE SHORTEST LIFESPAN—IT LIVES FOR ONLY ONE DAY.

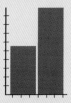

THE AVERAGE HUMAN LIFE EXPECTANCY HAS DOUBLED DURING THE LAST TWO CENTURIES.

FAST FACTS

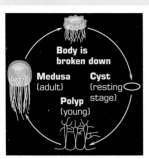

Body is broken down

Medusa (adult)

Cyst (resting stage)

Polyp (young)

The fingernail-size jellyfish *Turritopsis nutricula* is known as the "immortal jellyfish" because it can regrow its body. The adult, or medusa, starts its life cycle all over again as a young polyp. Unless it is eaten or dies of illness, it can keep doing this.

The number of growth rings on the shell shows how old the clam is.

Ocean quahog
507 years

Aldabra giant tortoise
255 years

The oldest known Aldabra giant tortoise's age was worked out by carbon dating the shell.

Bowhead whale
211 years

BY 2050, ABOUT 17% OF THE GLOBAL POPULATION WILL BE OVER 65 YEARS OLD.

THE WORLD'S OLDEST KNOWN ANIMAL DNA BELONGS TO AN ANCESTOR OF THE WOOLLY MAMMOTH.

Life-form data

LIFE ON EARTH

Mammals, birds, reptiles, amphibians, and fish are all **vertebrates** (animals with a backbone). Together, they make up just 3 percent of all animal species. **Invertebrates** (animals without a backbone) make up the remaining **97 percent**.

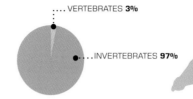

.... VERTEBRATES **3%**

...INVERTEBRATES **97%**

Nearly one quarter of all the animal species named so far are **beetles**, amounting to around **400,000 species**. In contrast, about 6,000 mammal species have been identified.

THE **BIG** ONES

The biggest land animals tower over the average human being.

MAN **6 FT** (1.8 M)

BIGGEST BIRD OSTRICH **9 FT** (2.75 M)

BIGGEST LAND ANIMAL ELEPHANT **13 FT** (4 M)

TALLEST LAND ANIMAL GIRAFFE **20 FT** (6 M)

BIRDS IN FLIGHT

A bird's **wing shape** depends on the **way it flies**. Birds that live in open areas have **long wings** suited to **gliding** and **soaring**. Birds that live in dense vegetation have **shorter wings** good for flying in **quick bursts**.

SPEED FLYING
Long, thin wings slip easily through the air

QUICK TAKE-OFF
Short, powerful wings flap fast

GLIDING
Long wings catch sea winds and allow bird to glide effortlessly

A NEW TYPE OF **MILLIPEDE** DISCOVERED IN 2020 HAD 1,306 LEGS—MORE THAN ANY OTHER ANIMAL.

EVERY TIGER AND ZEBRA HAS ITS OWN UNIQUE FURRY STRIPE PATTERN, BUT TIGERS HAVE STRIPED SKIN, TOO.

SAFETY IN NUMBERS

In 1889, a swarm of locusts with an area of **1,930 sq miles** (5,000 sq km) crossed the Red Sea in the Middle East. It is estimated to have weighed around **500,000 tons** (450,000 tonnes) and contained **250 billion locusts.**

The **African red-billed quelea** is the **most numerous** wild bird species on the planet and forms gigantic flocks. There are 1.5 billion breeding pairs.

Termite colonies can contain up to 3 million individuals. The **largest termite mound** ever discovered was 42 ft (12.8 m) tall.

Argentine ants live in giant groups known as **mega-colonies.** One of the **largest** is believed to stretch for 3,700 miles (6,000 km) along Europe's Mediterranean coast.

MICRO WORLD

A single gram of soil can contain **40 million bacteria.**

SOARING
Broad wings are good for soaring on gently rising air

RAPID MANEUVERS
Short, curved wings allow quick direction changes

TREES AND PLANTS

The **tallest trees** in the world are the **coast redwoods** of California. The tallest recorded specimen, named Hyperion, stands more than **380 ft** (116 m) high—the height of almost two and a half Statues of Liberty.

COAST REDWOOD **HYPERION 380 FT** (116 M)

Some species of kelp can grow up to **12 in** (30 cm) in a single day.

The rare Southeast Asian plant *Rafflesia arnoldii* (also known as the corpse flower) has the world's largest and possibly smelliest flower. It measures around **39 in** (1 m) across and stinks of rotting flesh.

The smallest flowering plant is *Wolffia globosa.* It measures just **0.02 in** (0.6 mm) long and **0.01 in** (0.3 mm) wide.

WOLFFIA (ACTUAL SIZE)

GIANT KELP

SARDINES FORM GIANT BAIT BALLS MEASURING UP TO 65 FT (20 M) WIDE TO CONFUSE PREDATORS.

IF SOME **SEA STARS** GET INJURED, THEY CAN GROW A NEW BODY FROM ONLY ONE ARM.

WHAT IS THE
FASTEST
RUNNER?

The fastest sprinters, running the 100 m in less than 10 seconds, reach their top speed usually during the 60–80 m stretch. If they could sustain this top speed throughout the race, they would run it in 8.4 seconds.

The **cheetah** is the **fastest land animal** but only over short distances. **Horses** are **slower** but can run **much farther** before they get tired.

27 mph
(43 kph)

WALKING ON WATER

Basilisk lizards can escape from predators by running across the surface of ponds and rivers. They can cover a distance of 65 ft (20 m) before they start to sink.

At its **top speed**, a cheetah would finish a 100 m sprint in around 3 seconds.

THE BASILISK LIZARD CAN RUN ACROSS WATER AT A SPEED OF AROUND 7 MPH (11 KPH).

ABOUT 200 SNAILS "RACE" TO THE FINISH LINE IN THE WORLD SNAIL RACING CHAMPIONSHIPS IN ENGLAND.

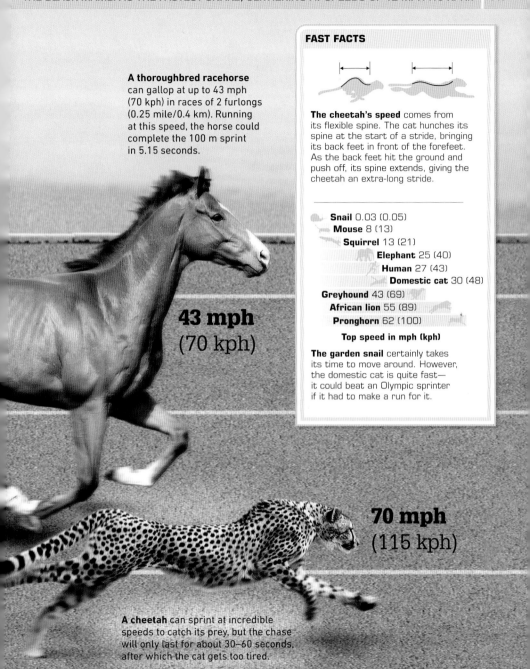

A thoroughbred racehorse can gallop at up to 43 mph (70 kph) in races of 2 furlongs (0.25 mile/0.4 km). Running at this speed, the horse could complete the 100 m sprint in 5.15 seconds.

43 mph
(70 kph)

FAST FACTS

The cheetah's speed comes from its flexible spine. The cat hunches its spine at the start of a stride, bringing its back feet in front of the forefeet. As the back feet hit the ground and push off, its spine extends, giving the cheetah an extra-long stride.

Snail 0.03 (0.05)
Mouse 8 (13)
Squirrel 13 (21)
Elephant 25 (40)
Human 27 (43)
Domestic cat 30 (48)
Greyhound 43 (69)
African lion 55 (89)
Pronghorn 62 (100)

Top speed in mph (kph)

The garden snail certainly takes its time to move around. However, the domestic cat is quite fast— it could beat an Olympic sprinter if it had to make a run for it.

70 mph
(115 kph)

A cheetah can sprint at incredible speeds to catch its prey, but the chase will only last for about 30–60 seconds, after which the cat gets too tired.

THE OLDEST MARATHON RUNNER IS FAUJA SINGH—HE RAN **13 MARATHONS** BETWEEN THE AGES OF 89 AND 101.

IN 2004, CHINESE RUNNER XU ZHENJUN COMPLETED THE BEIJING MARATHON RUNNING THE RACE **BACKWARD**.

WHAT ANIMAL CAN
JUMP THE FARTHEST?

The **snow leopard** of central Asia can **leap farther** than any other animal. It can cover more than **50 ft** (15 m) in a **single jump**.

GLIDING MAMMALS

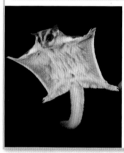

Some animals do not jump but can glide for long distances. For example, the sugar glider of Australia uses flaps of skin between its limbs to help it glide from tree to tree for 165 ft (50 m) or more.

30 ft (9 m)

29 ft 4.5 in (8.95 m)

10 ft (3 m)

The jerboa's long back legs help it jump more than 25 times its body length.

SNOW LEOPARDS USE THEIR **TAILS** FOR BALANCE WHEN JUMPING, BUT THEY ALSO DOUBLE UP AS BLANKETS!

THE HIMALAYAN JUMPING SPIDER IS ONLY 0.16 IN (4 MM) LONG, BUT IT CAN JUMP UP TO **25 TIMES** ITS OWN BODY LENGTH.

FAST FACTS

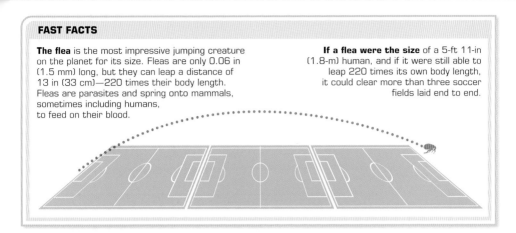

The flea is the most impressive jumping creature on the planet for its size. Fleas are only 0.06 in (1.5 mm) long, but they can leap a distance of 13 in (33 cm)—220 times their body length. Fleas are parasites and spring onto mammals, sometimes including humans, to feed on their blood.

If a flea were the size of a 5-ft 11-in (1.8-m) human, and if it were still able to leap 220 times its own body length, it could clear more than three soccer fields laid end to end.

When it jumps, the red kangaroo can reach a speed of more than 40 mph (64 kph) with single leaps of up to 30 ft (9 m).

The **snow leopard could** easily clear **seven large family cars in** one leap.

The human world record for men's long jump was set by US athlete Mike Powell in 1991.

Snow leopards live in mountain habitats where they leap to catch their prey of wild sheep and goats.

50 ft (15 m)

IN 1993, CUBAN ATHLETE JAVIER SOTOMAYOR LEAPT 8.04 FT (2.45 M) TO RECORD THE **HIGHEST JUMP** EVER BY A HUMAN.

IN **OLYMPIC TRAMPOLINING**, GYMNASTS ARE ALLOWED TO JUMP TO DIZZY HEIGHTS OF 33 FT (10 M).

WHAT IS THE
FASTEST FLYER?

In level flight, a **white-throated needletail** is the **fastest** bird in the air. It has a **top speed** of **105 mph** (170 kph).

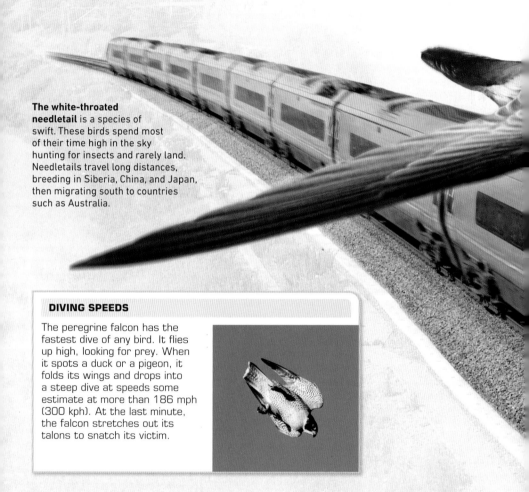

The white-throated needletail is a species of swift. These birds spend most of their time high in the sky hunting for insects and rarely land. Needletails travel long distances, breeding in Siberia, China, and Japan, then migrating south to countries such as Australia.

DIVING SPEEDS

The peregrine falcon has the fastest dive of any bird. It flies up high, looking for prey. When it spots a duck or a pigeon, it folds its wings and drops into a steep dive at speeds some estimate at more than 186 mph (300 kph). At the last minute, the falcon stretches out its talons to snatch its victim.

GREAT SNIPES TRAVELING AT SPEEDS OF 60 MPH (97 KPH) FLY FROM EUROPE TO AFRICA IN TWO DAYS.

THE RÜPPELL'S VULTURE CAN FLY AT 37,000 FT (11,280 M), WHICH IS HIGHER THAN MOST PASSENGER PLANES.

FAST FACTS

Although they walk with a slow waddle, ducks and waders are the fastest flying birds (other than swifts) that have been measured accurately. The great snipe has the fastest recorded migration.

Birds are the fastest fliers, but among other animals, free-tailed bats are the quickest. Dragonflies are among the speediest insects.

Common swift
69 mph (111 kph)

Great snipe (a wader)
60 mph (97 kph)

Eider duck
47 mph (76 kph)

Brazilian free-tailed bat
99 mph (160 kph)

Flying fish
37 mph (60 kph)

Dragonfly
31 mph (50 kph)

A white-throated needletail flies fast enough to keep up with a high-speed train.

Long, curved wings slip easily through the air.

This high-speed train has a maximum speed of 124 mph (200 kph), but on a scheduled passenger journey, it averages about 106 mph (171 kph), including stops.

A **WANDERING ALBATROSS** SOARS FOR DAYS ON END. ONE WAS RECORDED TRAVELING 3,730 MILES (6,000 KM) IN 12 DAYS.

THE **ALPINE SWIFT** SLEEPS IN FLIGHT BY LEAVING ONE EYE OPEN AND KEEPING HALF OF ITS BRAIN AWAKE.

WHAT IS THE
FASTEST
SWIMMER?

The **speediest swimmer**, the **sailfish**, could travel the length of an Olympic **swimming pool** in **1.6 seconds**— around **13 times faster** than the **human** record holder.

FAST FACTS

Sailfish
68 mph (110 kph)

Striped marlin
50 mph (80 kph)

Blue-fin tuna
44 mph (71 kph)

Blue shark
43 mph (69 kph)

Swordfish
40 mph (64 kph)

The fastest swimmers are all fish. At the top is the sailfish, which is an amazing 18 mph (30 kph) quicker than its nearest rival, the striped marlin.

Dall's porpoise
35 mph (56 kph)

California sea lion
25 mph (40 kph)

Octopus
25 mph (40 kph)

Gentoo penguin
22 mph (36 kph)

Leatherback turtle
21.5 mph (35 kph)

Some other sea animals swim fast. However, all are slower than the top five fastest fish, which have perfectly streamlined bodies with powerful muscles built for speed.

ONE HOUR OF SWIMMING BURNS 40% MORE CALORIES THAN CYCLING AND 30% MORE THAN RUNNING.

HUMPBACK WHALES MAKE ONE OF THE LONGEST MAMMAL MIGRATIONS, SWIMMING 4,970 MILES (8,000 KM).

LONG-DISTANCE SWIMMERS

Polar bears can swim very long distances. Scientists tracked one bear over a 427-mile (687-km) journey. It took nearly 10 days, and the bear didn't stop to eat or sleep.

5.3 mph (8.6 kph)

An Olympic swimmer can keep up his top sprint speed for only one length of the pool (164 ft/50 m).

67 mph (108 kph)

The fastest jet-skis can zoom across the water at about 12.5 times the speed of the Olympic swimmer.

A sailfish can dart through water at 68 mph (110 kph), faster than a jet-ski.

68 mph (110 kph)

A sailfish is a predator of the open ocean. It uses its speed and large dorsal fin to herd a shoal of fish into a ball. It then slashes its prey with its long bill.

THE DWARF SEAHORSE IS THE WORLD'S SLOWEST-MOVING FISH, REACHING SPEEDS OF ONLY 0.001 MPH (0.016 KPH).

SOME SEA SPONGES TRAVEL SLOWER THAN ANYTHING IN THE OCEANS, COVERING ABOUT 0.04 IN (1 MM) A DAY.

HOW DEEP CAN
ANIMALS GO?

Some animals can live at the bottom of **ocean trenches**. Even **air-breathing** animals, such as **elephant seals and Cuvier's beaked whales**, which must hold their breath, can **dive** to **extraordinary depths**.

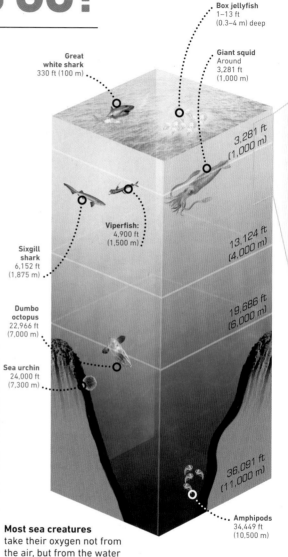

Box jellyfish
1–13 ft
(0.3–4 m) deep

Giant squid
Around
3,281 ft
(1,000 m)

Great white shark
330 ft (100 m)

3,281 ft
(1,000 m)

Viperfish:
4,900 ft
(1,500 m)

Sixgill shark
6,152 ft
(1,875 m)

13,124 ft
(4,000 m)

Dumbo octopus
22,966 ft
(7,000 m)

19,686 ft
(6,000 m)

Sea urchin
24,000 ft
(7,300 m)

36,091 ft
(11,000 m)

Amphipods
34,449 ft
(10,500 m)

LIVING LIGHTS

The deep-sea anglerfish has a fleshy rod growing from its head with a light on the end. In the complete darkness of the deep ocean, this glowing bait lures small fish and shrimp into the predator's gaping jaws.

Most sea creatures take their oxygen not from the air, but from the water around them. Animals, including shrimplike amphipods, can live in the deepest parts of the ocean.

PETAR KLOVAR ACHIEVED THE DEEPEST FREE DIVE WITHOUT ANY EQUIPMENT IN 2023, REACHING 419 FT AND 11 IN (128 M).

DIVER BUDIMIR ŠOBAT SET A NEW WORLD RECORD IN 2021 BY HOLDING HIS BREATH UNDERWATER FOR OVER 24 MINUTES.

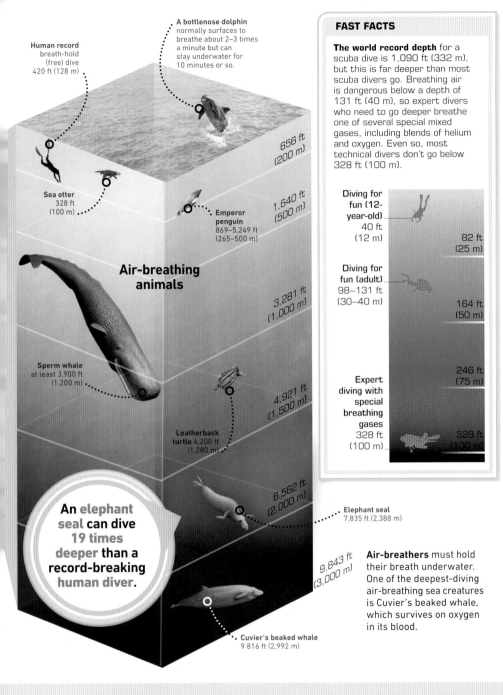

A bottlenose dolphin normally surfaces to breathe about 2–3 times a minute but can stay underwater for 10 minutes or so.

Human record breath-hold (free) dive 420 ft (128 m)

656 ft (200 m)

Sea otter 328 ft (100 m)

Emperor penguin 869–5,249 ft (265–500 m)

1,640 ft (500 m)

Air-breathing animals

3,281 ft (1,000 m)

Sperm whale at least 3,900 ft (1,200 m)

4,921 ft (1,500 m)

Leatherback turtle 4,200 ft (1,280 m)

6,562 ft (2,000 m)

Elephant seal 7,835 ft (2,388 m)

An **elephant seal** can dive **19 times deeper** than a record-breaking human diver.

9,843 ft (3,000 m)

Cuvier's beaked whale 9 816 ft (2,992 m)

FAST FACTS

The world record depth for a scuba dive is 1,090 ft (332 m), but this is far deeper than most scuba divers go. Breathing air is dangerous below a depth of 131 ft (40 m), so expert divers who need to go deeper breathe one of several special mixed gases, including blends of helium and oxygen. Even so, most technical divers don't go below 328 ft (100 m).

Diving for fun (12-year-old) 40 ft (12 m)

82 ft (25 m)

Diving for fun (adult) 98–131 ft (30–40 m)

164 ft (50 m)

246 ft (75 m)

Expert diving with special breathing gases 328 ft (100 m)

328 ft (100 m)

Air-breathers must hold their breath underwater. One of the deepest-diving air-breathing sea creatures is Cuvier's beaked whale, which survives on oxygen in its blood.

A CUVIER'S BEAKED WHALE STAYED UNDERWATER FOR NEARLY **4 HOURS**—THE LONGEST DIVE RECORDED FOR A MAMMAL.

THE **DUMBO OCTOPUS** IS THE DEEPEST-DIVING OCTOPUS, REACHING 22,965 FT (7,000 M) UNDERWATER.

HOW STRONG
IS AN ANT?

An **average-sized ant**, weighing about **0.0001 oz** (0.003 g), is able to **carry an object** that weighs **0.005 oz** (0.15 g)—that's **50 times** its **own weight**.

If a man were as strong as an ant, he would be able to lift three cars.

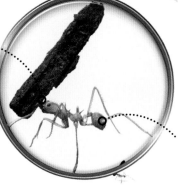

An ant carries objects in its mandibles—powerful jaws that it also uses to cut, crush, fight, and dig.

This leafcutter ant is 0.3 in (0.75 cm) long and can carry a piece of bark much larger than itself.

LEOPARD STRENGTH

When a leopard kills large prey, such as an antelope, it drags the body up a tree, away from hyenas and other scavengers. A male leopard can drag prey three times its weight—even a small giraffe—to a height of 20 ft (6 m).

Ants are strong because their muscles are bigger relative to the ant's overall size. Physics explains that an ant twice as long would have muscles four times stronger, but a body eight times heavier. This would make the muscles—and the ant—effectively half as strong.

LEAFCUTTER ANTS ARE FOUND IN CENTRAL AND SOUTH AMERICA AND IN PARTS OF TEXAS.

A LEAFCUTTER ANT COLONY CAN HAVE MILLIONS OF WORKERS CUTTING AND CARRYING **LEAVES** BACK TO THE NEST.

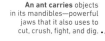

If a man weighing 176 lb (80 kg) could lift 50 times his own weight, that would be 4.4 tons (4 tonnes)—around the same as three cars.

FAST FACTS

6 house mice

Horned dung beetle

The male horned dung beetle deals with rival males by pushing them out of its burrow. Tests have shown that this species can pull 1,141 times its own body weight— the same as pulling six 0.7-oz (20-g) house mice.

Weightlifter Lasha Talakhadze

The largest weight lifted by a human is 588.6 lb (267 kg)— that's more than three times the weight of an average adult male. This was achieved by Lasha Talakhadze of Georgia in 2021. The women's weight-lifting record belongs to Tatiana Kashirina of Russia, who lifted 425.5 lb (193 kg) in 2014.

LEAFCUTTER ANTS HAVE CHAINSAWLIKE MANDIBLES, WHICH VIBRATE A THOUSAND TIMES PER SECOND.

TO AVOID GETTING LOST, LEAFCUTTER ANTS LEAVE BEHIND A SCENT TRAIL THAT THEY FOLLOW BACK TO THEIR NEST.

Animal data

LONG MIGRATIONS

6,000 MILES
(9,700 KM)

Leatherback turtles regularly swim **6,000 miles** (9,700 km) each way across the Pacific Ocean between their main feeding sites in California and their breeding areas in Indonesia.

3,000–4,500 MILES
(5,000–7,000 KM)

Eels in Europe have to travel **3,000–4,500 miles** (5,000–7,000 km) to their breeding grounds in the Sargasso Sea.

2,000 MILES
(3,200 KM)

Each year, **monarch butterflies** fly on average **2,000 miles** (3,200 km) between southern California and Mexico.

BIG MIGRATIONS

Every year on Africa's Serengeti Plains, more than **1.5 million wildebeest** undertake a **1,800-mile** (2,900-km) round trip in search for fresh grass. Around **250,000**, or **17%**, don't survive.

17%

Africa's biggest migration takes place each fall when around **8 million fruit bats** fly from the Democratic Republic of the Congo to neighboring Zambia to feast on newly ripened fruit.

SENSITIVE ANIMALS

▶ **Great white sharks** can detect blood in the water from up to **3 miles** (5 km) away. It's been estimated that they can smell a **single drop of blood** in

26 gallons
(100 liters) of water.

▶ **Jewel beetles** have an infrared sensor that allows them to **detect a forest fire** from up to **50 miles** (80 km) away. They then fly

toward the fire

and lay their eggs in the smoldering tree trunks.

▶ **Seals** have the most sensitive whiskers of any mammal and can **detect a fish** swimming more than **330 ft** (100 m) away.

▶ The heat-sensitive organs of **pit vipers** can detect **temperature** variations of just

0.003°F
(0.002°C).

FLYING FISH

Flying fish can soar over the water for up to **655 ft** (200 m)—the length of two average soccer fields.

A **SKUNK** CAN SPRAY ITS STINKY SCENT TO DETER PREDATORS AT LEAST 10 FT (3 M) AWAY.

DOGS AND **COWS** HAVE HAIRLESS SNOUTS THAT CREATE UNIQUE NOSE PRINTS!

KILLER CREATURES

▶ The sting of some **box jellyfish** is nearly always fatal unless treated immediately. Stings have killed more than **5,500 people** in the past 60 years.

▶ The venom of a **king cobra** can kill an adult human in **15–30 minutes**.

▶ A drop of venom from the **marbled cone snail** can kill **20 humans**, or one elephant.

FASTEST FLAPPERS

Some species of **hummingbird** can flap their wings at up to **80 times a second**—so *fast* it produces a faint humming sound.

HOW SNAKES MOVE

All snakes slide along the ground, but not all move in quite the same way. They have a few different ways of getting around on land:

CONCERTINA

SERPENTINE

SIDEWINDING

SLOWEST ANIMALS

While a **cheetah** may be able to race at up to **70 mph** (110 kph), some other creatures prefer to take their time getting from A to B.

GIANT TORTOISE⋯⋯⋯
0.2 MPH (0.3 KPH)

SEAHORSE
0.01 MPH
(0.016 KPH)

GARDEN SNAIL
0.03 MPH
(0.05 KPH)

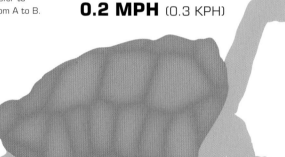

655 FT (200 M)

20 FT (6 M)

They can stay in the air for up to **45 seconds**, traveling at around **37 mph** (60 kph) and reaching heights of **20 ft** (6 m).

THE NEW CALEDONIAN CROW IS THE FIRST BIRD KNOWN TO MAKE **TOOLS** OUT OF STICKS AND USE THEM TO CATCH BUGS.

GREAT WHITE SHARKS CAN GO THROUGH A TOTAL OF ABOUT 30,000 TEETH DURING THEIR LIFETIME.

Feats of engineering

People are inventive and are always creating new things. Engineering—designing and making things—has given us powerful rockets, super-fast sports cars, spectacularly tall buildings, computers that can do billions of calculations per second, and much more.

One of the greatest engineering feats ever, Dubai's Palm Islands are among the biggest human-made islands in the world. Palm Jumeirah (pictured) is shaped like an enormous palm tree, covering an area of 2.2 sq miles (5.6 sq km)—more than the area of 800 soccer fields.

HOW FAST IS THE
FASTEST CAR?

The **fastest cars** in **motor sports** are **top fuel dragsters**, which reach **330 mph** (530 kph) from a **standing start** in less than **4 seconds**.

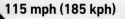

115 mph (185 kph)

231.5 mph (372.6 kph)

A family car, such as this Ford Focus, can barely go half as fast as a Formula 1 car.

The highest speed during a Formula 1 race was set by Juan Pablo Montoya during the 2005 Italian Grand Prix.

267.8 mph (431.1 kph)

AMERICAN SUPERCAR

Manufactured in the US, the Hennessey Venom GT holds a world record of 13.63 seconds for acceleration from 0–186 mph (0–300 kph). It has also reached a speed of 265.5 mph (427.4 kph).

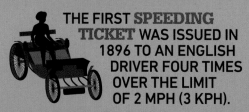

THE FIRST **SPEEDING TICKET** WAS ISSUED IN 1896 TO AN ENGLISH DRIVER FOUR TIMES OVER THE LIMIT OF 2 MPH (3 KPH).

IN 2008, AMPHIBIOUS VEHICLE **TONIC** CROSSED THE ENGLISH CHANNEL IN A RECORD TIME OF 1 HOUR AND 14 MINUTES.

FAST FACTS

The fastest cars of all are those designed to beat the world land speed record. During record attempts, cars are timed over two straight-line runs. Jet- and rocket-powered cars have held the main records since the 1960s, but other records exist for different types of vehicles, such as wind-powered.

Wind-powered
Horonuku 140.17 mph (225.58 kph)

Production road car
Bugatti Veyron 267.8 mph (431.1 kph)

Motorcycle
Ack Attack 376.4 mph (605.7 kph)

Wheel-driven
Vesco Turbinator 458.4 mph (737.7 kph)

Jet-propelled
Thrust SSC 763 mph (1,228 kph)

"Top fuel" is a class of car used in drag racing. These cars run on a mix of special, high-performance fuels and race on a strip that is only 1,000 ft (300 m) long. They can accelerate from 0–100 mph (0–160 kph) in less than a second and have to release parachutes behind them to help them brake.

330 mph (530 kph)

Reaching speeds of 267.8 mph (431.1 kph), the Bugatti Veyron Super Sport was one of the fastest production cars—that is, one built in numbers for people to drive on the road. Its successor, however, the Bugatti Chiron Supersport 300+, could reach speeds of 304.7 mph (490.4 kph). Only 30 models of the Supersport 300+ were built.

The fastest dragster reaches speeds 100 mph (160 kph) greater than any Formula 1 car.

THE US STATE OF NEVADA MADE HISTORY IN 2012 AS THE FIRST TO INTRODUCE **DRIVERLESS CARS** ON PUBLIC ROADS.

WHEN 216 VEHICLES RACED IN CALIFORNIA IN 2014, IT WAS THE WORLD'S BIGGEST **CAR RACE.**

The *Shanghai Maglev* covers 18½ miles (30 km) in less than 8 minutes.

STEAM POWER

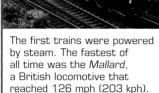

The first trains were powered by steam. The fastest of all time was the *Mallard*, a British locomotive that reached 126 mph (203 kph).

FAST FACTS

The fastest maglev train speeds have been reached by Japan's maglev test train, the *MLX01*. A manned rocket sled, however, has achieved even faster speeds.

Rocket sled

MLX01

632 mph (1,017 kph)

375 mph (603 kph)

168 mph (270 kph)

The yellow *TGV La Poste* was one of the world's fastest freight trains. It was used to transport mail in and out of Paris, France.

THE **STEAM-POWERED ROCKET** WAS THE FIRST VEHICLE TO TRAVEL FASTER THAN A HORSE IN 1829.

IN 2022, THE LONGEST PASSENGER TRAIN, CONSISTING OF **100 COACHES**, RAN THROUGH THE SWISS ALPS.

HOW FAST IS THE
FASTEST TRAIN?

The *Shanghai Maglev* is the **fastest passenger train** in the world. It can operate at speeds of up to **267 mph** (430 kph).

China's *Shanghai Maglev Train* is the fastest passenger train in service. Maglevs run on special tracks that lift them off the ground. They are smoother and quieter than ordinary trains.

The French TGV is the world's fastest wheel-based passenger train. It runs on high-speed tracks at up to 200 mph (320 kph) on regular services. A specially adapted version, the TGV V150, currently holds the world speed record of 357 mph (575 kph).

200 mph
(320 kph)

267 mph
(430 kph)

The track is called a guideway. When an electric current is sent through the guideway, magnets under the train generate a force that lifts and propels the train at high speed.

THE **FASTEST MODEL RAILWAY**, OSAKA BANPAKU TENJIMOKEI LINEAR MOTORCAR, REACHED 27.8 MPH (44.8 KPH) IN 2018.

THE QINGHAI-TIBET RAILWAY OPENED IN 2006 AS THE WORLD'S **HIGHEST RAILWAY**.

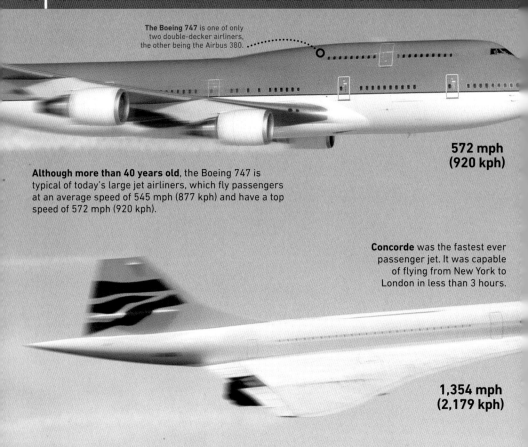

The **Boeing 747** is one of only
two double-decker airliners,
the other being the Airbus 380.

**572 mph
(920 kph)**

Although more than 40 years old, the Boeing 747 is
typical of today's large jet airliners, which fly passengers
at an average speed of 545 mph (877 kph) and have a top
speed of 572 mph (920 kph).

Concorde was the fastest ever
passenger jet. It was capable
of flying from New York to
London in less than 3 hours.

**1,354 mph
(2,179 kph)**

HOW FAST IS THE
FASTEST AIRCRAFT?

The **X-15** was the fastest **crewed airplane** to ever fly.
Its **record speed** of **4,534 mph** (7,297 kph) was set in
1967 and has never been beaten.

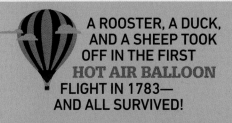

A ROOSTER, A DUCK,
AND A SHEEP TOOK
OFF IN THE FIRST
HOT AIR BALLOON
FLIGHT IN 1783—
AND ALL SURVIVED!

IN 1958, TWO PILOTS
FROM LAS VEGAS,
NEVADA, FLEW A
CESSNA C172 FOR
A RECORD-BREAKING
64 DAYS WITHOUT LANDING.

FAST FACTS

Flyer
30 mph
(48 kph)

Mallard duck
65 mph (105 kph)

The first aircraft to fly, the Wright brothers' Flyer, reached a top speed of 30 mph (48 kph). This is less than half the speed of a mallard duck, which flies at 65 mph (105 kph).

X-15—fastest manned aircraft — 4,534 mph (7,297 kph)

SpaceShipTwo—fastest passenger space plane — 2,600 mph (4,184 kph)

SR-71 Blackbird—fastest jet aircraft — 2,193 mph (3,529 kph)

Cessna Citation X—fastest passenger jet — 700 mph (1,126 kph)

Westland Lynx—fastest helicopter — 249 mph (400 kph)

The fastest aircraft fly to the edge of space. Tourists travel there in supersonic space planes.

The X-15 flew at nearly **eight times** the speed of a Boeing 747.

Bullet speeds vary, but a bullet from an M16 rifle is about the same as the fastest fighter jet.

2,125 mph (3,420 kph)

HTV-2

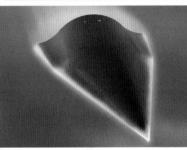

In 2011, an experimental plane, the uncrewed HTV-2, reached a speed of 13,000 mph (21,000 kph)—fast enough to travel from London to Sydney in less than an hour.

The X-15 couldn't take off like an ordinary plane. The experimental aircraft was carried by a bomber to its cruising altitude. Only then did the X-15 fire up its rocket engines.

4,534 mph (7,297 kph)

 IN 2019, A QUANTAS PLANE RECORDED THE WORLD'S LONGEST PASSENGER FLIGHT— IT WAS AIRBORNE FOR OVER **19 HOURS**.

 DESIGNED TO CARRY PASSENGERS INTO SPACE, SPACESHIPTWO IS TRANSPORTED TO ITS LAUNCH HEIGHT BY A CARRIER AIRCRAFT.

The LZ-130 *Graf Zeppelin II* could carry up to 72 passengers, plus a 40-man crew. With a top speed of 81 mph (131 kph), it had a range of 10,250 miles (16,500 km). The airship was filled with lighter-than-air gas and built to carry passengers across the Atlantic.

The **biggest Zeppelins** were **3 times longer** and **6 times wider** than a **Jumbo Jet**.

Graf Zeppelin

AIRBUS BELUGA

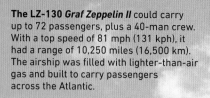

The Airbus Beluga is designed to carry large or awkwardly shaped cargo. This includes the parts for Airbus airliners, which are made in four different countries and then airlifted for assembly.

The gondola contained separate control and observation rooms, plus a central navigation area.

Huge windows, which could be opened during flights, ran the length of the passenger decks.

THE **FIRST POWERED AIRSHIP** WAS INVENTED BY ENGINEER HENRI GIFFORD IN 1852 AND TRAVELED 17 MILES (27 KM).

AROUND **1,200 AIRSHIPS** HAVE BEEN BUILT IN TOTAL, BUT ONLY ABOUT 25 REMAIN TODAY.

WHAT WAS THE BIGGEST AIRCRAFT?

At **804 ft** (245 m) **long**, the **Zeppelin airships** *Graf Zeppelin II* and *Hindenburg*, built in Germany in the 1930s, were the **largest aircraft** ever to take to the skies.

The **Boeing 747-400D**, launched in 1991, can carry up to 600 passengers, compared to the 72-person capacity of *Graf Zeppelin II*.

Each of the four engine cars were manned by a mechanic at all times during flights.

FAST FACTS

Airbus A380
238.6 ft (72.72 m)

Boeing 747-8 Intercontinental
250.7 ft (76.4 m)

Antonov An-225
275.6 ft (84 m)

The **Antonov An-225** was the world's longest airplane—longer than the Airbus 380 and the Boeing 747. Although it was designed to carry the Russian space shuttle Buran, it was also used for transporting outsized cargo items.

THE **LARGEST HELICOPTER** IN HISTORY WAS THE TWIN-ROTOR SOVIET MIL V-12, WITH A TAKE-OFF WEIGHT OF 115 TONS (105 TONNES).

THE WORLD'S LARGEST CARGO AIRCRAFT, THE **ANTONOV AN-225**, WAS AS BIG AS A SOCCER FIELD.

HOW FAST IS THE FASTEST
WATERCRAFT?

A record of **318 mph** (511 kph) was set by a
speedboat, the ***Spirit of Australia***, in 1978.
It has yet to be beaten.

The *Spirit of Australia* **is five times faster than** *Hydroptère*.

FAST FACTS

Sometimes you can go almost as fast
on a board as you can on a boat. The
kitesurfing record of 65.1 mph (104.8 kph)
is close behind the fastest sailing craft,
Sailrocket 2, and is faster than
Hydroptère's 60.8 mph (97.9 kph). The
fastest windsurfer is nearly as fast.

Windsurfer
61.3 mph (98.7 kph)

Kitesurfer
65.1 mph (104.8 kph)

Vestas Sailrocket 2
75.3 mph (121.2 kph)

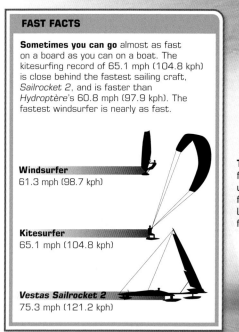

Under each side float of
Hydroptère is a foil, or wing.
Once the boat is at a certain
speed, the foils lift it so that it
almost flies above the water.

l'Hydroptère

The jet ski's small size,
fast speed, and ease of
use make it ideal
for use by police,
lifeguards, and
fun seekers.

67 mph (108 kph)

THE BOAT WAS
DESIGNED BY
WARBY, WHO USED
WOOD FOR
BUILDING HIS
SPEEDBOAT.

THE *SPIRIT OF AUSTRALIA* WAS
POWERED BY A JET ENGINE THAT WAS
DEVELOPED FOR FIGHTER JETS
IN THE 1940S.

Hydroptère was one of the fastest sailing vessels ever made. The boat was built for speed and its crew aimed to break sailing world speed records.

60.8 mph (97.9 kph)

The *Spirit of Australia* was a jet-powered speedboat driven by Australian Ken Warby.

318 mph (511 kph)

FOSSEYS

KW2N

THE **TOOLS** USED BY WARBY WERE THOSE HE HAD ON HAND—SAW, SANDER, AND DRILL!

MANY OF THE PEOPLE WHO HELPED WARBY **BUILD** HIS BOAT WERE FRIENDS AND VOLUNTEERS.

FAST FACTS

Harmony of the Seas
1,187 ft (362 m)

Knock Nevis
1,504 ft (458 m)

USS *Enterprise* (aircraft carrier)
1,123 ft (342 m)

Azzam
590 ft (180 m)

Statue
of Liberty
305 ft
(93 m)

The longest supertanker ever was *Knock Nevis*, which was broken up in 2010. The USS *Enterprise* is the longest naval ship in the world, but it is still shorter than one of the largest cruise ships, the *Harmony of the Seas*. The *Harmony* is nearly as tall as the Statue of Liberty and twice the length of the *Azzam*, the largest private yacht.

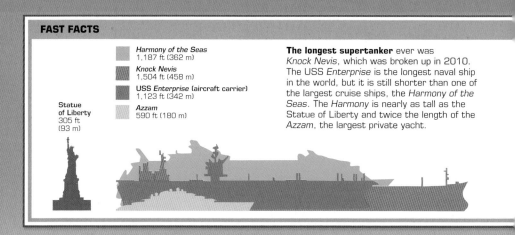

HOW BIG IS A
SUPERTANKER?

The **TI *Oceania*** is the same **length** as **29 US school buses** placed **end-to-end.**

The *Oceania* and its three sister ships are the largest ever oil tankers to have double hulls—the bottom and sides of the ship have two watertight walls to prevent oil spills in the event of an accident.

A **FULLY LOADED** SUPERTANKER SITS ABOUT TWO-THIRDS UNDERWATER AT A DEPTH OF 75 FT (23 M).

SUPERTANKERS TAKE OIL FROM WHERE IT IS EXTRACTED TO OIL REFINERIES.

The anchor from the *Knock Nevis* weighed 40 tons (36 tonnes)—more than seven African bull elephants. It is the only part of the ship that remains.

HARMONY OF THE SEAS

One of the world's biggest cruise ship, the *Harmony of the Seas*, can carry up to 5,479 passengers and 2,100 crew. Cruise ships like this resemble floating towns with restaurants, cinemas, and stores.

At **1,246 ft** (380 m) **long** and **223 ft** (68 m) **wide**, the **TI *Oceania*** is the **biggest supertanker** afloat today. It can carry **3 million barrels of oil** and when full weighs **486,764 tons** (441,585 tonnes).

TI *Oceania* has a top speed of 16.5 knots (19 mph/31 kph). At this speed, it would take 44 seconds for the entire ship to pass someone watching from the shore.

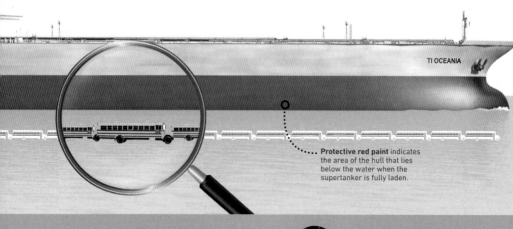

TI OCEANIA

Protective red paint indicates the area of the hull that lies below the water when the supertanker is fully laden.

A SUPERTANKER TAKES UP TO **20 MINUTES** TO REACH A COMPLETE STOP.

THE *HARMONY OF THE SEAS* CRUISE SHIP EVEN HAS A FULL-SIZE BASKETBALL COURT!

HOW MUCH CAN A
SHIP CARRY?

The **supersized container ship MSC *Oscar*** can carry **19,224** standard-size **containers**. It is **1,297 ft** (395.4 m) **long**.

The bridge (from where the captain controls the ship) sits far forward so containers can be stacked high without the captain losing visibility.

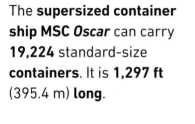

Standard containers are used to transport all kinds of goods all over the world, from fruit to clothes and TVs. Each standard container is 20 ft (6.1 m) long and 8 ft (2.44 m) wide and can be lifted from the ship to fit directly onto a truck or train.

CONTAINERS WERE DESIGNED SO THAT THEY COULD BE STACKED UP LIKE **BUILDING BLOCKS.**

IN 1997, A CONTAINER SHIP SPILLED ITS CARGO OF **5 MILLION** LEGO® BRICKS, WHICH ARE STILL BEING FOUND TODAY!

FAST FACTS

The biggest tankers can carry even more cargo than container ships. The *Knock Nevis* supertanker was 1,504 ft (458 m) long and could hold 4.1 million barrels of oil—enough to fill 260 Olympic swimming pools.

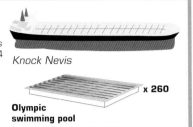

Knock Nevis

x 260

Olympic swimming pool

BLUE MARLIN

Heavy-lift ships, such as the *Blue Marlin*, transport huge structures such as oil rigs or aircraft carriers. The ship can submerge its deck to duck under the structure, then raise it again once the cargo has been loaded.

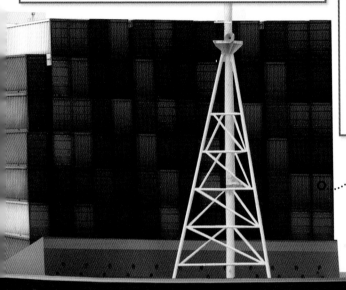

MSC OSCAR

If every container was fully loaded, the ship would be too heavy to sail. It can carry a maximum 217,554 tons (197,362 tonnes), or 11 tons (10 tonnes) per container.

At 240 ft (73 m) tall, the MSC *Oscar* is as tall as a 25-story building. It is also 13 times longer than a blue whale, and five buses could park end-to-end across its 194-ft (59-m) width. It sails between Asia and Europe.

Fully loaded, MSC *Oscar* could carry 38,448 cars or 920 million cans of soup.

IN 2002, *TRICOLOUR* WAS CARRYING NEARLY 3,000 LUXURY CARS WHEN IT COLLIDED WITH ANOTHER SHIP AND SANK.

CONTAINER SHIP *EVER GIVEN* RAN AGROUND AND BLOCKED THE SUEZ CANAL IN 2021, CAUSING A QUEUE OF NEARLY 400 SHIPS.

HOW POWERFUL WAS THE
SPACE SHUTTLE?

The **Shuttle's** three engines and two rocket boosters produced **6.8 million lb** (3.1 million kg) of **thrust**.

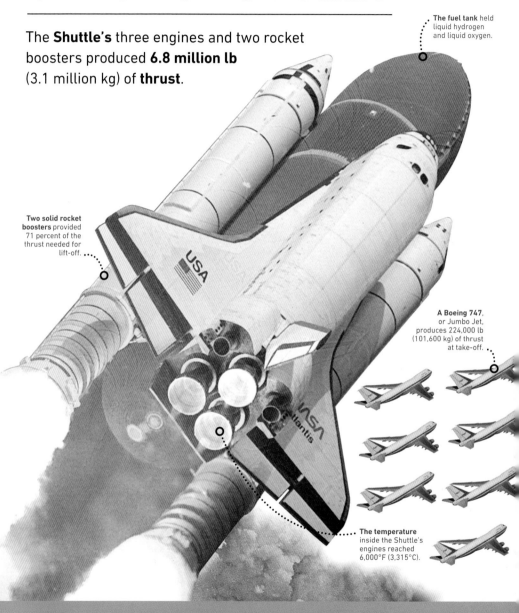

The fuel tank held liquid hydrogen and liquid oxygen.

Two solid rocket boosters provided 71 percent of the thrust needed for lift-off.

USA

NASA atlantis

A Boeing 747, or Jumbo Jet, produces 224,000 lb (101,600 kg) of thrust at take-off.

The temperature inside the Shuttle's engines reached 6,000°F (3,315°C).

 THE SPACE SHUTTLES WERE **NAMED** AFTER SHIPS USED IN EXPLORATION: *ATLANTIS, CHALLENGER, COLUMBIA, DISCOVERY,* AND *ENDEAVOUR.*

 THE SPACE SHUTTLE REACHED EARTH'S ORBIT IN **EIGHT AND A HALF MINUTES.**

FAST FACTS

The Space Shuttle's three engines could burn the equivalent of 2.4 swimming pools of liquid fuel in a minute—that's 1,000 gallons (3,785 liters) a second.

Swimming pool 33 x 20 ft (10 x 6 m)

Space Shuttle

Thrust SSC 1

The Space Shuttle took just under 40 seconds to reach a speed of 621 mph (1,000 kph). However, the holder of the world land speed record, the Thrust SSC 1 rocket car, reached this speed in 16 seconds—less than half the time taken by the Shuttle.

The **Space Shuttle had** the **same power as 31** Jumbo Jets.

HEAVY LIFTING

The Shuttle weighed around 2,200 tons (2,000 tonnes) at launch. Most of that came from the rockets and fuel needed to propel it fast enough to escape the pull of gravity and enter orbit.

BETWEEN 1981 AND 2011, NASA'S SPACE SHUTTLES MADE MORE THAN 21,000 **ORBITS OF EARTH.**

THE **SPACE SHUTTLE PROGRAM** SAW 306 MEN AND 49 WOMEN FROM A TOTAL OF 16 COUNTRIES TAKE FLIGHT.

HOW FAR HAVE PEOPLE BEEN
INTO SPACE?

In **1970**, the crew members of the **Apollo 13 Moon mission** were the first to travel a record distance of **248,655 miles** (400,171 km) **from Earth**. That record, however, was broken in **2022**, when **NASA's Orion spacecraft** reached the distance of **270,000 miles** (435,000 km) **from Earth**.

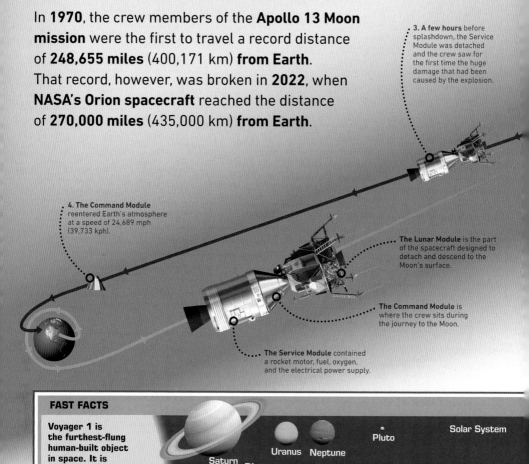

3. A few hours before splashdown, the Service Module was detached and the crew saw for the first time the huge damage that had been caused by the explosion.

4. The Command Module reentered Earth's atmosphere at a speed of 24,689 mph (39,733 kph).

The Lunar Module is the part of the spacecraft designed to detach and descend to the Moon's surface.

The Command Module is where the crew sits during the journey to the Moon.

The Service Module contained a rocket motor, fuel, oxygen, and the electrical power supply.

FAST FACTS

Voyager 1 is the furthest-flung human-built object in space. It is **15 billion miles** (24 billion km) from Earth and in 2012 became the first craft to leave our Solar System.

Solar System

Pluto

Uranus   Neptune

Saturn   **Distance**
Earth   Solar System distances are measured in AU (Astronomical Units). One AU is the distance between Earth and the Sun.

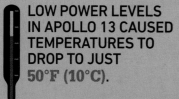

LOW POWER LEVELS IN APOLLO 13 CAUSED TEMPERATURES TO DROP TO JUST 50°F (10°C).

THE THREE **APOLLO ASTRONAUTS** WERE CONFINED IN A SPACE THAT WAS NO BIGGER THEN A MINIVAN.

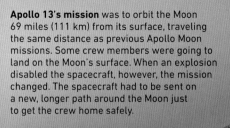

Apollo 13's mission was to orbit the Moon 69 miles (111 km) from its surface, traveling the same distance as previous Apollo Moon missions. Some crew members were going to land on the Moon's surface. When an explosion disabled the spacecraft, however, the mission changed. The spacecraft had to be sent on a new, longer path around the Moon just to get the crew home safely.

2. Apollo 13 flew 164 miles (264 km) past the Moon before swinging back on its return path.

The distance from Earth reached by Apollo 13 was equivalent to 10 circuits of Earth's equator.

1. The craft was 204,000 miles (329,000 km) from Earth and almost 56 hours into its flight when an explosion crippled the Service Module's fuel, power, and oxygen supplies. The mission to land on the Moon had to be aborted.

MISSION CONTROL

In the Apollo 13 Service Module, a fan in an oxygen tank short-circuited, causing the tank to catch fire and explode. Mission controllers on Earth worked out that they could use the Moon's gravity to bring the craft back on course for home.

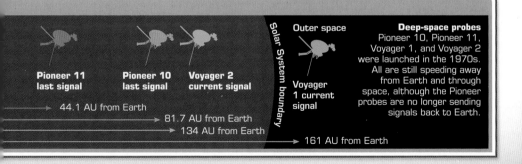

Pioneer 11
last signal

Pioneer 10
last signal

Voyager 2
current signal

Solar System boundary

Outer space

Voyager 1
current
signal

Deep-space probes
Pioneer 10, Pioneer 11, Voyager 1, and Voyager 2 were launched in the 1970s. All are still speeding away from Earth and through space, although the Pioneer probes are no longer sending signals back to Earth.

44.1 AU from Earth

81.7 AU from Earth

134 AU from Earth

161 AU from Earth

 ORION CARRIES UP TO SIX ASTRONAUTS— THE CREW MODULE IS 50% BIGGER THAN THE APOLLO CRAFT.

 COMPUTERS ON BOARD ORION ARE ABOUT 20,000 TIMES FASTER THAN ON THE APOLLO CRAFT.

HOW HIGH WAS
THE HIGHEST PARACHUTE JUMP?

In 2014, American **Alan Eustace** broke the **world record** when he leapt from a balloon **135,889 ft (41,419 m) above the Earth.**

At the edge of space, the air pressure is less than 2 percent of what it is at sea level. You would need to wear a pressurized suit to prevent yourself from blacking out as you fell.

Wispy cirrus clouds can form as high as 46,000 ft (14,000 m).

2012 FREEFALL RECORD

The previous record holder, Austrian Felix Baumgartner, reached a speed of 844 mph (1,358 kph) during his freefall in 2012. He was the first person to break the sound barrier without the help of a vehicle.

The **skydive** was roughly **four times the height** of a cruising airliner.

Airliners usually cruise at around 33,000 ft (10,000 m).

Most parachute jumps are made from less than 14,100 ft (4,300 m). Even at this height, you will freefall at around 100 mph (160 kph).

IT TOOK EUSTACE JUST OVER **2 HOURS** TO REACH THE HEIGHT OF 135,889 FT (41,419 M).

THE **BALLOON** WAS 450 FT (137 M) TALL—LONGER THAN THE LENGTH OF A SOCCER FIELD.

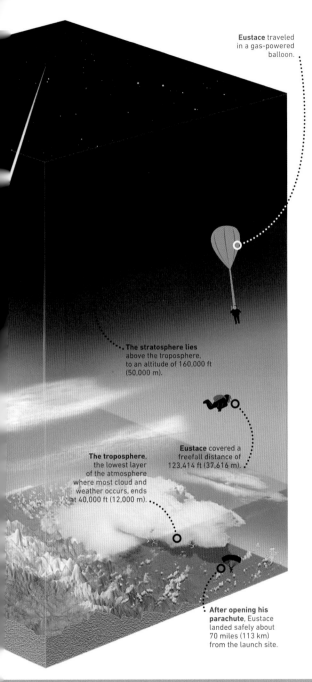

Eustace traveled in a gas-powered balloon.

The stratosphere lies above the troposphere, to an altitude of 160,000 ft (50,000 m).

Eustace covered a freefall distance of 123,414 ft (37,616 m).

The troposphere, the lowest layer of the atmosphere where most cloud and weather occurs, ends at 40,000 ft (12,000 m).

After opening his parachute, Eustace landed safely about 70 miles (113 km) from the launch site.

Jumping from the stratosphere is very risky. The air is far too thin to breathe, and Eustace could only carry a 15-minute supply of air with him for the descent. He also hung from the balloon and used a small explosive device to free himself when he reached the edge of space.

FAST FACTS

Only rocket planes are able to fly high in the atmosphere because the lack of oxygen prevents jet engines from working.

International Space Station 1,312,335 ft (400,000 m)

Passenger spacecraft SpaceShipTwo 360,000 ft (110,000 m)

Highest jet airplane SR-71 Blackbird 80,000 ft (24,000 m)

Highest rocket airplane X-15 354,200 ft (108,000 m)

Passenger airliner 33,000 ft (10,000 m)

EUSTACE'S **SUIT** WAS SPECIFICALLY MADE FOR HIM—IT WAS BASED ON THOSE WORN BY ASTRONAUTS.

THE ENTIRE DESCENT TOOK A TOTAL OF **15 MINUTES**.

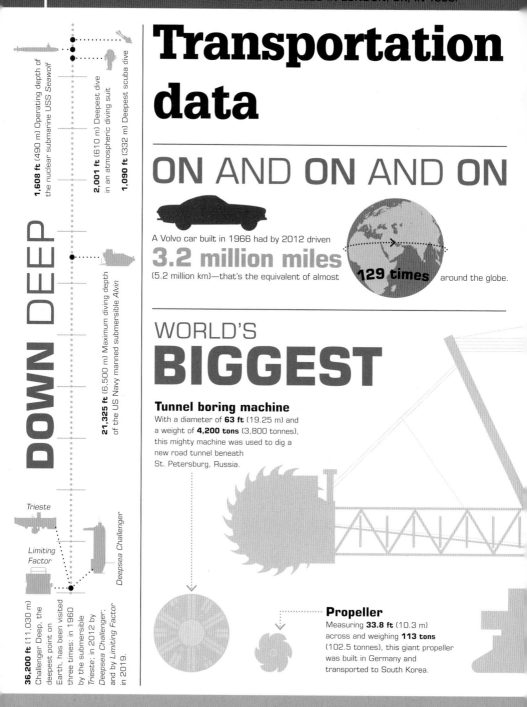

DOWN DEEP

1,608 ft (490 m) Operating depth of the nuclear submarine USS *Seawolf*

2,001 ft (610 m) Deepest dive in an atmospheric diving suit.

1,090 ft (332 m) Deepest scuba dive

21,325 ft (6,500 m) Maximum diving depth of the US Navy manned submersible *Alvin*

Trieste

Limiting Factor

Deepsea Challenger

36,200 ft (11,030 m) Challenger Deep, the deepest point on Earth, has been visited three times: in 1960 by the submersible *Trieste*; in 2012 by *Deepsea Challenger*; and by *Limiting Factor* in 2019.

Transportation data

ON AND ON AND ON

A Volvo car built in 1966 had by 2012 driven

3.2 million miles

(5.2 million km)—that's the equivalent of almost **129 times** around the globe.

WORLD'S
BIGGEST

Tunnel boring machine
With a diameter of **63 ft** (19.25 m) and a weight of **4,200 tons** (3,800 tonnes), this mighty machine was used to dig a new road tunnel beneath St. Petersburg, Russia.

Propeller
Measuring **33.8 ft** (10.3 m) across and weighing **113 tons** (102.5 tonnes), this giant propeller was built in Germany and transported to South Korea.

THERE ARE ABOUT 1 BILLION **BICYCLES** WORLDWIDE, WITH 450 MILLION BICYCLES IN CHINA ALONE.

THE MOST EXPENSIVE **CAR** IS A 1955 MERCEDES-BENZ 300 SLR UHLENHAUT. IT SOLD FOR $145 MILLION (£114 MILLION).

LONGEST NONSTOP PASSENGER FLIGHTS

18 HOURS, 45 MINUTES

Singapore to Newark, NJ **9,523 miles** (15,325 km)

18 HOURS, 50 MINUTES

Singapore to New York: **9,537 miles** (15,348 km)

LONGEST TRAIN

The world's longest train had **682 cars** and eight locomotives. It was used just once to haul iron ore in Australia in 2001 and it measured **4.57 miles** (7.353 km) long. That's the length of **8.8 Burj Khalifas** laid end-to-end.

TOTAL AMOUNT OF RAILWAY TRACK IN THE WORLD

More than **770,262 miles** (1,239,615 km)—more than three times the distance from Earth to the Moon.

The three countries with the most railway track are the US, China, and Russia. Between them, they have just under one third of all the world's track.

US: **139,679 miles** (224,792 km)

China: **75,186 miles** (121,000 km)

Russia: **53,400 miles** (86,000 km)

Land vehicle

An enormous excavator used in the German mining industry, the **Bagger 293** is **738 ft** (225 m) long and **315 ft** (96 m) high and weighs **15,652 tons** (14,200 tonnes). It can fill 2,400 coal wagons a day.

Human

Animal

The blue whale measures **100 ft** (30 m) long.

CHINA'S SHANGHAI METRO IS THE WORLD'S LONGEST RAIL NETWORK WITH 515 MILES (830 KM) OF TRACK AND 508 STATIONS.

NASA'S LUNAR ROVING VEHICLE WAS THE FIRST CREWED VEHICLE TO EXPLORE THE MOON'S SURFACE IN 1971.

HOW SMALL IS THE
TINIEST COMPUTER?

A **miniscule computer** less than the size of a grain of rice can **read temperatures, take pictures,** and **record pressure readings**. It is small enough to be **injected into the body** or to **detect pockets of oil** in rock.

FAST FACTS

Computers are getting smaller each year. In 1993, to do 143 GFLOPS (143 billion calculations a second), you needed a computer 5 ft (1.5 m) tall and 25 ft (8 m) long. Only 20 years later, just four laptops exceeded this performance.

Moore's Law, invented by Gordon Moore, a founder of Intel, suggests that computers double in performance every two years. In fact, the average speed of the 500 fastest computers in the world more than doubled every two years during the decade 2002–2012.

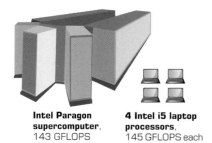

Intel Paragon supercomputer,
143 GFLOPS

4 Intel i5 laptop processors,
145 GFLOPS each

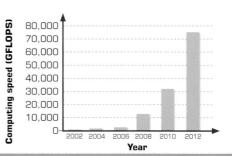

Computing speed (GFLOPS) vs Year

AT LEAST HALF OF ALL THE WORLD'S EMAILS ARE SPAM OR JUNK AND NEVER OPENED.

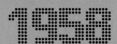

THE FIRST COMPUTER GAME WAS CREATED IN 1958—TWO PLAYERS PRESSED BUTTONS TO HIT A LIGHT ACROSS A COURT.

This miniature device, called the Michigan Micro Mote, could have lots of different uses. As well as being inserted into the body to measure temperature or pressure or used to find oil, it could also help us avoid losing things in our homes. Sticking the tiny computers onto keys or wallets could help us find these items using a central system.

The computer doesn't have a battery, but uses light as a source of power. It doesn't need to be natural sunlight, so the computer can work indoors.

It would take about 150 of these computers to fill a thimble.

MICROPROCESSORS

Computers became a lot smaller in 1971 with the invention of the microprocessor—the silicon chip that is the central processing unit of a computer. A silicon chip has a miniature electrical circuit printed on it. These printed circuits are smaller every year.

THE SPACE BAR IS THE MOST USED KEY ON A COMPUTER KEYBOARD, FOLLOWED BY THE LETTER "E."

IN 1964, THE VERY FIRST COMPUTER MOUSE WAS CARVED OUT OF WOOD AND FEATURED ONLY ONE BUTTON.

HOW MANY BOOKS CAN YOU FIT
ON A FLASH DRIVE?

A **1-terabyte (TB)** flash drive can store the text of **1 million books**. One terabyte is just over **1 million megabytes** (MB), or more than **1 trillion bytes**.

A flash drive weighs less than 1.1 oz (30 g) but can hold 1 TB of data. Flash memory can be erased and reprogrammed thousands of times.

A **1-TB flash drive could store 1 million 200-page books.**

FAST FACTS

The Library of Congress in Washington, DC, is the biggest library in the world, containing 35 million books. All the text in those books could be stored on nine 4-TB hard disks.

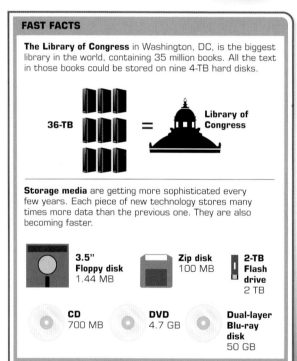

36-TB   =   Library of Congress

Storage media are getting more sophisticated every few years. Each piece of new technology stores many times more data than the previous one. They are also becoming faster.

3.5" **Floppy disk** 1.44 MB

Zip disk 100 MB

2-TB Flash drive 2 TB

CD 700 MB

DVD 4.7 GB

Dual-layer Blu-ray disk 50 GB

★ THE NAME "FLASH MEMORY" ORIGINATED WHEN A COMPUTER WORKER COMPARED DELETING DATA IN ONE GO TO A CAMERA FLASH.

FLASH DRIVES DON'T HAVE MOVING PIECES AND CAN CONTINUE WORKING EVEN AFTER BEING DAMAGED.

ATOMIC DATA STORAGE

Seen here under a powerful electron microscope is the world's smallest data storage unit. Scientists have used just 12 iron atoms to hold one bit (the basic unit of information), and 96 atoms to hold a byte. A hard disk still needs half a billion atoms per byte.

A STANDARD FLASH DRIVE CAN LAST UP TO 100,000 USES, SO OVERUSE IS VERY RARELY A PROBLEM!

FLASH DRIVES NOW COME IN ALL STYLES, INCLUDING BOTTLE OPENERS, DRINK CANS, AND COMPANY LOGOS.

Computer data

ON THE GO ...

Smartphones aren't just for making phone calls and taking pictures! They have a **range of hardware and software functions**, which you can operate using a touchscreen.

YOU CAN ...

Browse the Internet

Play games

Listen to music

Make payments

... AND MUCH MORE!

The world's first smartphone—**IBM's Simon**—was released in 1994. It weighed a hefty 18 oz (510 g)—nearly three times more than a modern smartphone. It could send and receive emails and faxes and had a calendar, address book, calculator, and notebook.

THE WORLD WIDE WEB (WWW)

Computer scientist **Tim Berners-Lee** created the **first website** in 1991 for the European Organization for Nuclear Research (CERN). He invented a system that enabled computer users to find out information by **clicking on a link**. Today, there are **billions of web pages**!

75%

of people don't scroll past the first page of the search results!

SUPER
COMPUTER

It takes about **6,000 gallons** (22,712 liters) of water per minute to cool the world's fastest supercomputer, **Frontier.** The pumps are so powerful, they could fill an Olympic-sized swimming pool in 30 minutes.

PERCENTAGE OF **PEOPLE ONLINE** IN EACH CONTINENT IN 2023

NORTH AMERICA
94%

EUROPE
89%

ASIA
67%

SOUTH AMERICA
80%

AFRICA
43%

OCEANIA
70%

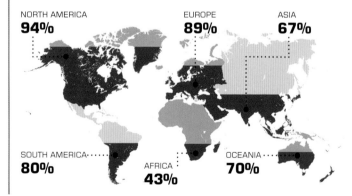

IN 1976, APPLE LAUNCHED ITS FIRST PRODUCT, A BASIC COMPUTER CALLED APPLE 1.

TIM BERNERS-LEE'S FIRST WEBSITE WAS: HTTP://INFO.CERN.CH. IT WAS LAUNCHED ON AUGUST 6, 1991.

FLOOR
SPACE

ENIAC, the world's **first electronic computer**, was built in 1946. It covered **1,798 sq ft** (167 sq m) and could perform **5,000** calculations per second.

Today's fastest computer, **Frontier**, covers **7,300 sq ft** (678 sq m) and performs **2 quintillion** calculations per second.

MOON
LANDING

The **computer** on board the **Apollo 11** spacecraft that landed on the Moon in 1969 had just **72 kb** of memory, of which just **4 kb** was RAM.

COMPUTER VS.
HUMAN

Computers with **artificial intelligence (AI)** carry out complicated tasks, including playing chess. The world's best human chess players have even been beaten by chess computers.

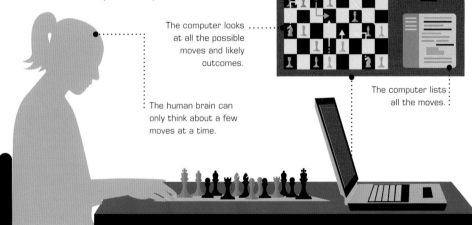

The computer looks at all the possible moves and likely outcomes.

The human brain can only think about a few moves at a time.

The computer lists all the moves.

HUMAN CHESS PLAYER

COMPUTER CHESS PLAYER

@YOU'VE
GOT MAIL

The **first email** was sent by computer engineer Ray Tomlinson in Cambridge, Massachusetts, in **1971**.

CODING **PIONEER**

The **first computer programmer** was 19th-century mathematician **Ada Lovelace**, who recognized that a computer could follow instructions (an algorithm) to complete calculations.

IN 2023, GOOGLE.COM WAS THE WORLD'S MOST VISITED WEBSITE WITH OVER 94 BILLION MONTHLY VISITS.

THE AVERAGE PERSON WORLDWIDE HAS MORE THAN 6 HOURS OF SCREEN TIME A DAY, MOSTLY ON MOBILE PHONES.

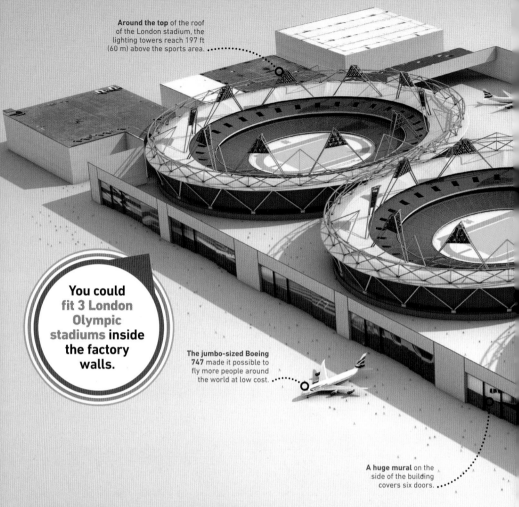

Around the top of the roof of the London stadium, the lighting towers reach 197 ft (60 m) above the sports area.

You could **fit 3 London Olympic stadiums** inside the factory walls.

The jumbo-sized Boeing 747 made it possible to fly more people around the world at low cost.

A huge mural on the side of the building covers six doors.

HOW BIG IS THE
BIGGEST BUILDING?

Used for putting airplanes together, **Boeing's Everett Factory** in Seattle, Washington, has a **volume** of **472 million cu ft** (13.4 million cu m).

WHEN THE FACTORY WAS BUILT, THE BOEING 747 WAS THE BIGGEST AIRCRAFT IN THE WORLD.

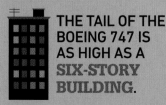

THE TAIL OF THE BOEING 747 IS AS HIGH AS A SIX-STORY BUILDING.

The Everett factory is so huge, you could fit the entire Disneyland or 55 soccer fields inside. Beneath the plant are 2.3 miles (3.7 km) of pedestrian tunnels.

PRODUCTION LINE

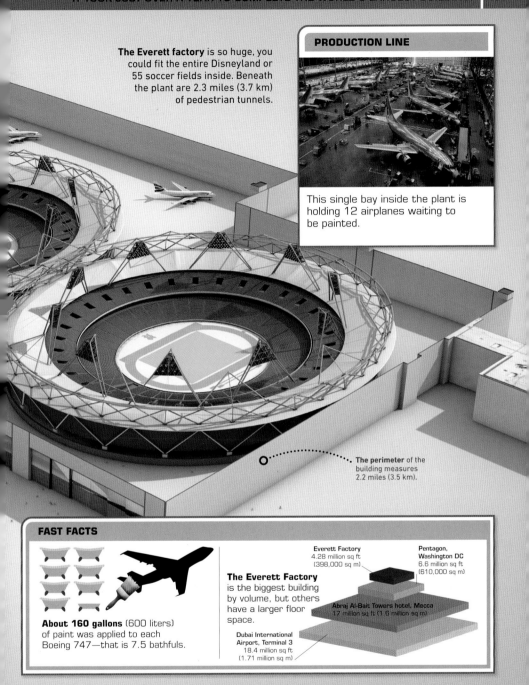

This single bay inside the plant is holding 12 airplanes waiting to be painted.

The perimeter of the building measures 2.2 miles (3.5 km).

FAST FACTS

About 160 gallons (600 liters) of paint was applied to each Boeing 747—that is 7.5 bathfuls.

The Everett Factory is the biggest building by volume, but others have a larger floor space.

Everett Factory
4.28 million sq ft
(398,000 sq m)

Pentagon, Washington DC
6.6 million sq ft
(610,000 sq m)

Abraj Al-Bait Towers hotel, Mecca
17 million sq ft (1.6 million sq m)

Dubai International Airport, Terminal 3
18.4 million sq ft
(1.71 million sq m)

THERE ARE ABOUT 1,300 **BICYCLES** ON HAND TO HELP WORKERS MOVE AROUND THE VAST COMPLEX.

THE SIX SIDE DOORS ARE 82 FT (25 M) HIGH—IT TAKES ABOUT **5 MINUTES** TO OPEN ONE DOOR!

FAST FACTS

Millau bridge deck
40,000 tons
(36,000 tonnes)

5 x
Eiffel Towers

The bridge's steel deck contains enough steel to make five Eiffel towers. The deck was built in a total of 2,200 separate sections, which were welded together into two halves, then pushed out toward each other from opposite sides of the valley.

Each of the longest cables on the viaduct is strong enough to withstand the maximum thrust of eight Boeing 747s.

The **Millau Viaduct** carries a stretch of the road that leads from Montpellier, in southern France, to Paris. The bridge is 8,070 ft (2,460 m) long and was opened in 2004.

HOW TALL IS THE
TALLEST
BRIDGE?

The **Millau Viaduct**, which spans the valley of the river **Tarn** in **France**, is the **tallest bridge** in the world. Its **largest mast** is **1,125 ft** (343 m) above the base, where it meets the **valley floor**.

BUILT IN c.850 BCE, THE ARKADIKO BRIDGE IN TURKEY IS CONSIDERED THE OLDEST DATABLE BRIDGE.

THE HONG KONG–ZHUHAI–MACAU BRIDGE, WHICH SPANS 34 MILES (55 KM), IS THE LONGEST SEA-CROSSING BRIDGE.

There are **seven masts** of different heights across the valley. Each holds 11 pairs of stays (metal cables). The stays support the road deck.

The Empire State Building measures 1,250 ft (381 m) to its roof. If it sat in the bottom of the valley, the roof would be just 40 ft (12 m) above the bridge's tallest point.

LONGEST BRIDGE

The world's longest bridge is the Danyang–Kunshan Grand Bridge in China at 102.4 miles (164.8 km) long. The bridge is part of the Beijing–Shanghai High-Speed Railway. Two more of the world's five longest bridges are part of the same railway line.

The **Millau Viaduct is almost as tall as the Empire State Building**.

THE GOLDEN GATE BRIDGE IN SAN FRANCISCO, CALIFORNIA, IS THE MOST PHOTOGRAPHED BRIDGE IN THE WORLD.

SOME COUNTRIES HAVE WILDLIFE BRIDGES THAT ENABLE ANIMALS TO SAFELY CROSS BUSY ROADS!

FAST FACTS

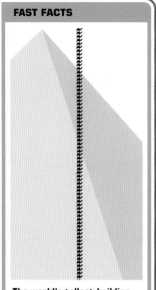

The world's tallest building for 3,800 years, the Great Pyramid measures 481 ft (147 m), the same height as a stack of 70 camels.

The largest of the stones that make up the Great Pyramid weigh 69 tons (63 tonnes), or the weight of 20 African bull elephants.

HOW HEAVY IS
THE GREAT PYRAMID?

Egypt's **Great Pyramid of Giza**, one of Earth's oldest buildings, weighs **5,750,100 tons** (5,216,400 tonnes).

The **Great Pyramid weighs the same as** 16 Empire State Buildings.

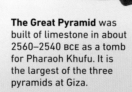

The Great Pyramid was built of limestone in about 2560–2540 BCE as a tomb for Pharaoh Khufu. It is the largest of the three pyramids at Giza.

IT TOOK MORE THAN 20 YEARS AND AT LEAST 20,000 LABORERS TO **BUILD** THE GREAT PYRAMID OF GIZA.

THE **PYRAMID** WAS BUILT WITH GREAT ACCURACY—THE BASE IS ALMOST PERFECTLY FLAT!

The Empire State Building has a steel frame covered with concrete, brick, stone, and glass. Unlike the pyramid, it isn't solid, but has 102 floors of mainly office space.

To the top of its spire, the Empire State Building measures 1,453 ft (443 m) tall. When it was finished in 1931, it was the world's tallest building.

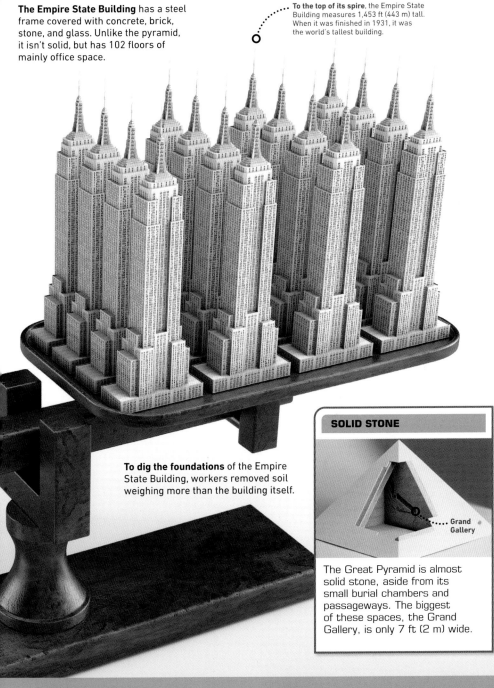

To dig the foundations of the Empire State Building, workers removed soil weighing more than the building itself.

SOLID STONE

Grand Gallery

The Great Pyramid is almost solid stone, aside from its small burial chambers and passageways. The biggest of these spaces, the Grand Gallery, is only 7 ft (2 m) wide.

MORE THAN 2.3 MILLION BLOCKS OF STONE WERE USED TO COMPLETE PHARAOH KHUFU'S PYRAMID.

THE PYRAMID IS PROTECTED BY THE GREAT SPHINX STATUE, WITH THE HEAD OF A HUMAN AND THE BODY OF A LION.

HOW DEEP
CAN WE DIG?

The **deepest ever human-made hole** is the **Kola Superdeep Borehole**, which was begun in 1970. **By 1994**, when the project was abandoned, the hole was **7.62 miles (12.262 km) deep**.

The center of Earth is 3,959 miles (6,371 km) below the surface. A journey there would begin with traveling through between 3 and 44 miles (5 and 70 km) of crust. Below this are the dense rocks of the mantle and the liquid-metal outer core. Each of these layers is more than 1,200 miles (2,000 km) thick. The inner core is a solid ball of iron and nickel about 794 miles (1,278 km) thick.

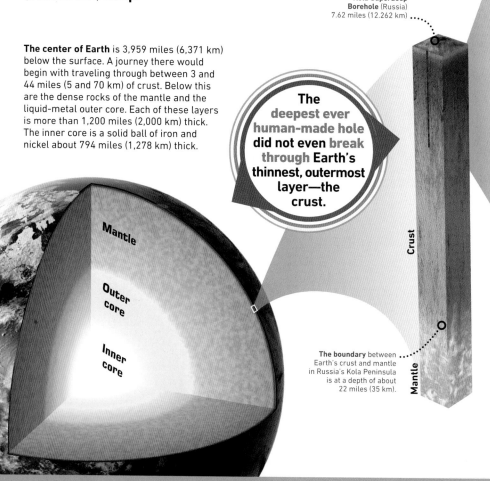

Kola Superdeep Borehole (Russia)
7.62 miles (12.262 km)

The deepest ever human-made hole did not even break through Earth's thinnest, outermost layer—the crust.

Mantle

Outer core

Inner core

Crust

The boundary between Earth's crust and mantle in Russia's Kola Peninsula is at a depth of about 22 miles (35 km).

Mantle

DRILLING A 9 IN (23 CM) HOLE TO A DEPTH OF 7.62 MILES (12.262 KM) TOOK NEARLY **20 YEARS**.

THE BOREHOLE IS ABOUT **15 TIMES** THE HEIGHT OF THE TALLEST BUILDING IN THE WORLD: DUBAI'S BURJ KHALIFA.

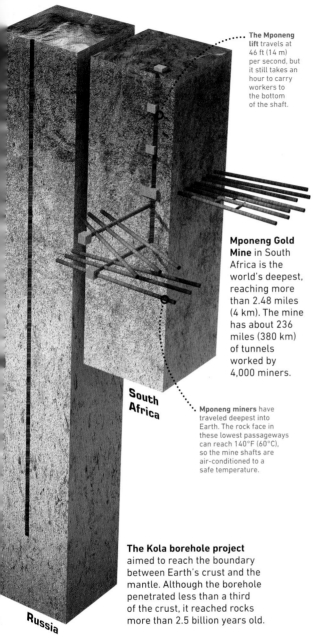

The Mponeng **lift** travels at 46 ft (14 m) per second, but it still takes an hour to carry workers to the bottom of the shaft.

Mponeng Gold Mine in South Africa is the world's deepest, reaching more than 2.48 miles (4 km). The mine has about 236 miles (380 km) of tunnels worked by 4,000 miners.

South Africa

Mponeng miners have traveled deepest into Earth. The rock face in these lowest passageways can reach 140°F (60°C), so the mine shafts are air-conditioned to a safe temperature.

The Kola borehole project aimed to reach the boundary between Earth's crust and the mantle. Although the borehole penetrated less than a third of the crust, it reached rocks more than 2.5 billion years old.

Russia

FAST FACTS

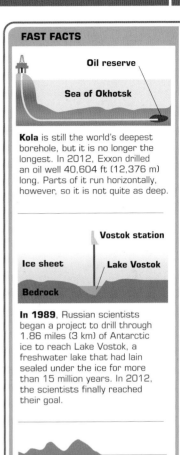

Oil reserve

Sea of Okhotsk

Kola is still the world's deepest borehole, but it is no longer the longest. In 2012, Exxon drilled an oil well 40,604 ft (12,376 m) long. Parts of it run horizontally, however, so it is not quite as deep.

Vostok station

Ice sheet   **Lake Vostok**

Bedrock

In 1989, Russian scientists began a project to drill through 1.86 miles (3 km) of Antarctic ice to reach Lake Vostok, a freshwater lake that had lain sealed under the ice for more than 15 million years. In 2012, the scientists finally reached their goal.

Continental crust

Oceanic crust

Upper mantle

Scientists almost broke through the crust where is it particularly thin, at less than 3.4 miles (5.5 km), in the ocean off Costa Rica. Oceanic crust is always thinner than continental crust, which forms Earth's landmasses and is 15–45 miles (25–70 km) thick.

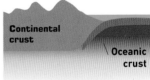

WORK STOPPED WHEN TEMPERATURES REACHED 356°F (180°C), WHICH WOULD HAVE MELTED THE EQUIPMENT.

THE BOREHOLE IS KNOWN AS THE "WELL TO HELL" BY LOCALS AND REMAINS COVERED BY A METAL LID.

HOW MUCH GOLD
IS THERE?

From **ancient times** to the **present day**, experts estimate that just **188,800 tons** (171,300 tonnes) of **gold** have been dug out of the ground.

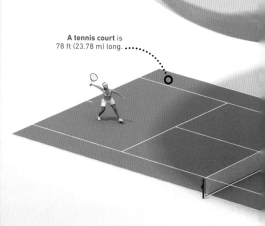

A ball the width of a tennis court might not sound big enough for 188,800 tons (171,300 tonnes) of gold, but gold is a very heavy metal. Two solid gold house bricks would weigh as much as an adult person.

GOLD NUGGETS

A nugget is a naturally occurring lump of gold. Most nuggets are small—but not all of them. This top shelf shows a model of the Welcome Stranger nugget, found in Australia in 1869 and weighing about 172 lb (78 kg).

A tennis court is 78 ft (23.78 m) long.

SINCE ANCIENT TIMES, GROUND-UP GOLD WAS USED BY ARTISTS TO MAKE GOLD PAINT.

THE INCA PEOPLE BELIEVED GOLD WAS SWEAT FROM THE SUN AND CONSIDERED IT SACRED.

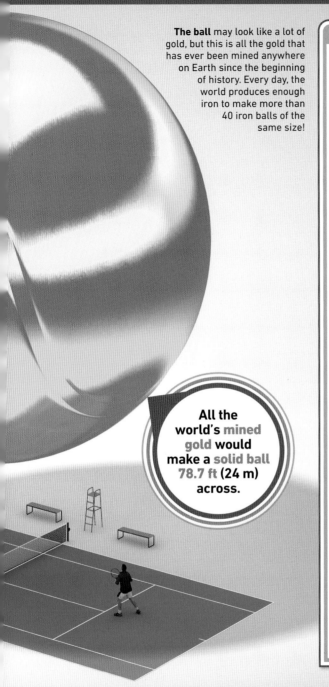

The ball may look like a lot of gold, but this is all the gold that has ever been mined anywhere on Earth since the beginning of history. Every day, the world produces enough iron to make more than 40 iron balls of the same size!

All the world's **mined gold** would make a **solid ball 78.7 ft (24 m)** across.

FAST FACTS

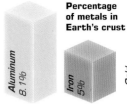

Percentage of metals in Earth's crust

- Aluminum 8.1%
- Iron 5%
- Gold 0.0000004%

Gold is much rarer than iron or aluminum, which make up large percentages of Earth's crust. Gold is valuable because it is so rare, but also because its shiny beauty never rusts or tarnishes.

Gold left in the ground

Mined Gold

We have already mined about 80 percent of the world's recoverable gold. Only 51,000 tons (46,000 tonnes) of the gold left in the ground could be extracted with existing technology.

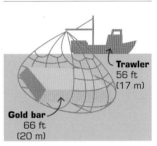

Trawler 56 ft (17 m)

Gold bar 66 ft (20 m)

Sea water contains dissolved gold. There may be up to 16,500 tons (15,000 tonnes) of it in the world's oceans. If this gold could be extracted, it would make a bar measuring 66 ft x 33 ft x 13 ft (20 m x 10 m x 4 m).

THE WORLD'S **OLDEST COINS** WERE MADE FROM ELECTRUM—A MIX OF GOLD AND SILVER.

SCIENTISTS USE A THIN LAYER OF GOLD FOIL ON AN ASTRONAUT'S **VISOR** TO REFLECT THE SUN'S GLARE.

Buildings data

BIGGEST CITIES BY POPULATION

1. **TOKYO, JAPAN** 37.3 MILLION

2. **NEW DELHI, INDIA** 25.9 MILLION

3. **SHANGHAI, CHINA** 23.5 MILLION

4. **MEXICO CITY, MEXICO** 21.3 MILLION

5. **SÃO PAULO, BRAZIL** 20.9 MILLION

6. **MUMBAI, INDIA** 19.3 MILLION

FASTEST ELEVATOR

Located in the Shanghai Tower skyscraper in China, it can travel at

3,543 ft

(1,080 m) per minute, or just less than 40 mph (65 kph).

LARGEST SCHOOL

City Montessori
Lucknow, India

With a total of **1,050 classrooms** located on **20 campuses** across the city, the school has more than **51,000 pupils** aged between **3 and 17**.

WORLD'S L O N G E

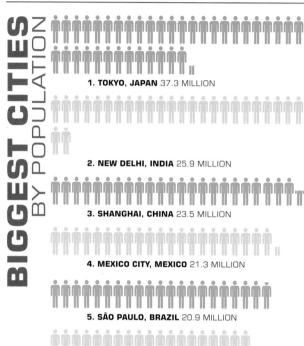

THE BAWABET DIMASHQ RESTAURANT IN DAMASCUS, SYRIA, IS THE LARGEST RESTAURANT— IT HAS ROOM FOR MORE THAN 6,000 DINERS.

THE WORLD'S TALLEST STATUE IS THE STATUE OF UNITY IN GUJARAT, INDIA, WHICH TOWERS TO 597 FT (182 M).

WORLD'S MOST **NORTHERLY**

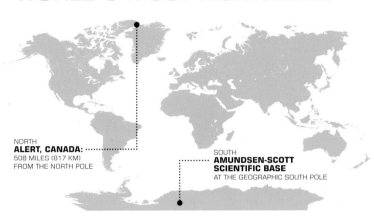

NORTH
ALERT, CANADA:
508 MILES (817 KM)
FROM THE NORTH POLE

SOUTH
**AMUNDSEN-SCOTT
SCIENTIFIC BASE**
AT THE GEOGRAPHIC SOUTH POLE

AND **SOUTHERLY** SETTLEMENTS

WORLD'S
HIGHEST

HIGHEST CITY ·············>
LA RINCONADA
PERU
16,732 FT
(5,100 M)
ABOVE SEA LEVEL

HIGHEST CAPITAL CITY
LA PAZ ·············>
BOLIVIA
11,942 FT
(3,640 M)
ABOVE SEA LEVEL

LARGEST STORE

Shinsegae Centum City
Department Store, South Korea
Spread over **18 floors**, it has an
overall floor area of **3.16 million sq ft**
(293,904 sq m)—that's more than
40 average-sized soccer fields.

LONGEST TUNNELS

LONGEST CONTINUOUS TUNNEL
DELAWARE AQUEDUCT, US
85 MILES (137 KM)

LONGEST UNDERSEA TUNNEL
SEIKAN TUNNEL, JAPAN
34 MILES (54 KM)
AT **787 FT** (240 M)

LONGEST ROAD TUNNEL
LAERDAL TUNNEL, NORWAY
16 MILES (25 KM)

LOWEST CAPITAL CITY
BAKU
AZERBAIJAN
92 FT
(28 M)
BELOW SEA LEVEL

LOWEST CITY
JERICHO
WEST BANK,
MIDDLE EAST
853 FT
(260 M)
BELOW SEA LEVEL

SEA LEVEL

S T ROAD BRIDGES

1. BANG NA EXPRESSWAY, THAILAND
177,000 FT (54,000 M)

2. QINGDAO HAIWAN BRIDGE, CHINA
136,417 FT (41,580 M)

3. LAKE PONTCHARTRAIN CAUSEWAY, US
126,122 FT (38,442 M)

AND
LOWEST
CITIES

THE WORLD'S BIGGEST
DOORS AT THE NASA
VEHICLE ASSEMBLY
BUILDING IN FLORIDA
MEASURE 456 FT
(139 M) TALL.

SWITZERLAND'S NIESEN
TREPPENLAUF IS THE
WORLD'S LONGEST
STAIRCASE WITH
A STAGGERING
11,674 STEPS.

INDEX

ACKNOWLEDGMENTS

Dorling Kindersley would like to thank: Scarlett O'Hara for proofreading; Carron Brown for indexing; Oliver Brown for editorial assistance and additional text; Steve Hoffman for fact checking; Astha Singh, Abhimanyu Adhikary, and Adarsh Tripathi for design assistance; Vikram Singh for creative retouching; and Deepak Negi and Manpreet Kaur for picture research assistance.

The publisher would like to thank the following for their kind permission to reproduce their photographs:

(Key: a-above; b-below/bottom; c-center; f-far; l-left; r-right; t-top)

2 Corbis: STScI / NASA (tr). 3 Corbis: National Geographic Society / Richard Nowitz (tl); Michele Westmorland (tc). Dreamstime.com: Pictac (bl); Haider Yousuf (tr). 4-5 Corbis: STScI / NASA. 6-7 Alan Friedman / avertedimagination.com: (c). 6 Institute for Solar Physics: SST / Göran Scharmer / Mats Löfdahl (bl). 7 NASA: GSFC / F. Espenak (cl/Reproduced five times). 8 NASA: Hinode / XRT (clb). 9 Dreamstime.com: Elisanth (cra/Reproduced four times, cr/moons); Stanalin (tr, crb, cr). 10-11 Pascal Henry, www.lesud.com. 10 NASA: (clb). 12-13 Science Photo Library: Mark Garlick. 12 Dorling Kindersley: London Planetarium (fcl). Dreamstime.com: Elisanth (cl). 13 NASA: (bc). 14 Dreamstime.com: Mmeeds (clb). 16 NASA: ESA and H. Hammel, MIT (clb). 18 Dreamstime.com: Bruno Metal (bc). com: Jabiru (bl). 22 NASA: ESA, J. Hester, A. Loll (ASU) (tl). 24 NASA: CXC / SAO / F. Seward (cl). 27 NASA Goddard Space Flight Center: Tom Zagwodzki (tr). 28 NASA: (bl). 28-29 Science Photo Library: Chris Butler (c). 29 ESA / Hubble: S. Beckwith (STScI) and the HUDF Team (br). Getty Images: Azem Ramadani (tl). Science Photo Library: Mark Garlick (cr). 32-33 Corbis: National Geographic Society / Richard Nowitz. 34 123RF.com: Igor Dolgov (bc). 35 NASA: Visible Earth / Jeff Schmaltz (cr). 37 Dreamstime.com: Asdf_1 (tc). 38 Dreamstime.com: Ericsch (bl). 39 Shutterstock.com: Petr Born (tl). 40 Dreamstime.com: Maxwell De Araújo Rodrigues (cla/Reproduced seven times). 41 Getty Images: National Geographic (cr). 42 Corbis: Galen Rowell (bl). 44 NASA: JPL / University of Arizona (clb). 46 Corbis: Arctic-Images (clb). 48 Corbis: Charles & Josette Lenars (bc). 49 Getty Images: Mike Copeland (crb). 50-51 Getty Images: National Geographic. 52 Corbis: Paul Souders (clb). 54 Corbis: Science Faction / Norbert Wu (clb). 57 Corbis: Nippon News / Aflo / Newspaper / Mainichi (rb). 58 Getty Images: Paul Souders

(bl). 60 NSIDC: USGS, W. O. Field (1941) and B. F. Molnia (2004) (clb). 61 Dreamstime.com: Maxwell De Araújo Rodrigues (cr/Reproduced five times). 63 Dreamstime.com: Elina Yakhontova (bc). 64 Getty Images: Katsumasa Iwasawa (tl). 64-65 Dreamstime.com: Stockshoppe (c). 65 Dreamstime.com: Laraslk (crb). 66 Corbis: Visuals Unlimited (c). 67 Dreamstime.com: Pictac (bc). 70 Getty Images: (bl). 70-71 Getty Images: Hulton Archive. 72 Corbis: Ocean (clb). 72-73 Corbis: Ikon Images / Jurgen Ziewe (c). 74-75 Corbis: Michele Westmorland. 76 Corbis: TempSport / Jerome Prevost (cl). Dreamstime.com: Alexandr Mitiuc (clb, bc, br). 76-77 Dorling Kindersley: Zygote Media Group (c). 77 Dreamstime.com: Alexandr Mitiuc (bl, bc, crb). 78 Getty Images: Vince Michaels (br). Science Photo Library: GJLP / CNRI (cl). 79 Corbis: 3d4Medical.com (bl). 80 Corbis: Science Photo Library / Steve Gschmeissner (cl). 83 Shutterstock.com: Granate Art (bl). 84 Corbis: Visuals Unlimited (clb). 85 Corbis: Minden Pictures / Flip Nicklin (bc). Dorling Kindersley: Natural History Museum, London (bl). 88 naturepl.com: Doc White (tc). 90 Dorling Kindersley: Bedrock Studios (tc). Dreamstime.com: Ibrahimyogurtcu (bc). 90-91 Dorling Kindersley: Andrew Kerr (c). 92-93 Dorling Kindersley: Andrew Kerr (c). 93 Dorling Kindersley: Jon Hughes and Russell Gooday (cr). 94 Science Photo Library: Peter Chadwick (cl). 96-97 Science Photo Library: Christian Darkin. 98 Paul Nylander, http://bugman123.com. 99 Alamy Images: Michal Cerny (tc). 100 Alamy Images: Louise Murray (clb). 102-103 Dreamstime.com: Bruce Crandall (c). 104 Alamy Images: Kevin Elsby (t). 105 Alamy Images: Rolf Nussbaumer Photography (tr). 105 naturepl.com: Karine Aigner (cl). Dreamstime.com: Pictac (t). 107 Dorling Kindersley: Natural History Museum, London (tr). 108 Dreamstime.com: Nilanjan Bhattacharya (bc). Otorohanga Zoological Society (1980): (bl). 110 Dr. Avishai Teicher: (clb). 110 Dreamstime.com: Nostone (bl). 112 Alaska Fisheries Science Center, NOAA Fisheries Service: (crb). Pearson Asset Library: Lord and Leverett / Pearson Education Ltd. (cb). Dreamstime.com: John Anderson (cl); Ispace (fbl, bl, bc, br, fbr). 113 Dreamstime.com: Ispace (bl, bc, br). Photoshot: NHPA / Paul Kay (cra). 116 Getty Images: Jose Luis Pelaez Inc. (c); Visuals Unlimited, Inc. / Joe McDonald (clb). 117 Corbis: Minden Pictures / Suzi Eszterhas (b). 118 Corbis: imagebroker / Konrad Wothe (cb). Dreamstime.com: Juri Bizgajmer (b/Reproduced four times). Getty

Images: Joe McDonald (cl). 119 Corbis: Wally McNamee (fclb); Robert Harding World Imagery / Thorsten Milse (clb). Dreamstime.com: Juri Bizgajmer (b/Reproduced three times). Getty Images: Daniel J. Cox (crb). 120 Science Photo Library: Jim Zipp (bc). 120-121 Alamy Images: Matthew Clarke. 122-123 Alamy Images: Transtock Inc. (c). 123 Corbis: Paul Souders (tr). Dreamstime.com: F9photos (tl). Getty Images: Ronald C. Modra (bl). 124 Alamy Images: Bluegreen Pictures / David Shale (clb). Corbis: Wim van Egmond (crb). Dreamstime.com: Ferdericb (ca). naturepl.com: David Shale (cr). 125 Dorling Kindersley: Dolphin Research Center, Grassy Key, Florida, www.dolphins.org (ca); Natural History Museum, London (cl, cb). Getty Images: AFP (cla). 126 Alamy Images: Duncan Usher (cl). Dreamstime.com: Isselee (br). 128 Dreamstime.com: Georgii Dolgykh (clb); Jezper (tl); Goce Risteski (cl). 130-131 Dreamstime.com: Haider Yousuf. 132 Corbis: epa / ULI DECK (crb); Transtock (clb). Dreamstime.com: Raja Rc (c). Getty Images: Bill Pugliano (cla). 132-133 Corbis: Chris Crisman. 133 Corbis: Icon SMI / J. Neil Prather (cl). 134-135 Alstom Transport: P. Sautelet (c). Corbis: Imaginechina (clb). 134 Alamy Images: Sagaphoto.com / Gautier Stephane (c). Getty Images: SSPL (cl). 136 Corbis: George Hall (t). 136-137 Getty Images: Marvin E. Newman (c). 137 Alamy Images: LM (crb). NASA: (b). 138 Alamy Images: DIZ Muenchen GmbH, Sueddeutsche Zeitung Photo (c). Dreamstime.com: Brutusman (clb). 139 Dreamstime.com: Rui Matos (cl). 140-141 Getty Images: AFP / MARCEL MOCHET. 140 Getty Images: Bryn Lennon (b). 143 Dreamstime.com: Richard Koele (b). Alamy Stock Photo: Newzulu (tr). 144 123RF.com: 3ddock (clb). Dreamstime.com: Chernetskiy (b/Reproduced two times). 144-145 A. P. Moller/Maersk: (c). 145 Dockwise: (tr). 146 Alamy Images: Dennis Hallinan (c). 147 Corbis: Morton Beebe (c/Boeing). NASA: (br). 149 NASA: (cb). 150 Science Photo Library: Ria Novosti (clb). 154-155 Corbis: Science Faction / Louie Psihoyos (finger). 155 University of Michigan: Martin Vloet (c). Alamy Images: David J. Green (crb). 156 Dreamstime.com: Marekp (ct). 157 Sebastian Loth, CFEL Hamburg, Germany: (br). 162-163 Getty Images: Charles Bowman (c). 163 Getty Images: Edward L. Zhao (tr). 168 Alamy Images: Giffard Stock (clb). 169 Getty Images / iStock: ioanmasay (bc).

All other images
© Dorling Kindersley
For further information see:
www.dkimages.com